AHMO Power

AHMO Power

◆

The Story Of the 1977 Texas 2A State Champion Wylie Pirates

Brian Honea

iUniverse, Inc.
New York Lincoln Shanghai

AHMO Power
The Story Of the 1977 Texas 2A State Champion Wylie Pirates

All Rights Reserved © 2004 by Brian Honea

No part of this book may be reproduced or transmitted in any form or by any means, graphic, electronic, or mechanical, including photocopying, recording, taping, or by any information storage retrieval system, without the written permission of the publisher.

iUniverse, Inc.

For information address:
iUniverse, Inc.
2021 Pine Lake Road, Suite 100
Lincoln, NE 68512
www.iuniverse.com

ISBN: 0-595-30810-4

Printed in the United States of America

This book is for all the players, coaches, trainers, cheerleaders, band members, students, parents and everyone who helped make that magical season happen for the Wylie Pirates. It is dedicated to my wife, Gloria; to my parents; to Kristin, Joel and Sean; to Annie and Pearl; and to Wayne Tyson, Kenneth Ard and Beverly Gothard. I would like to thank everyone who consented interviews and helped in any other way with the gathering of information for this work.

On the cover: A team photograph of the 1977 Wylie Pirates, taken late in the season at Garland Memorial Stadium. Pictured are, front row, from left: Coach Bruce King, 62-Chuck Edge, 31-Wayne Mayberry, 3-Wendell Collins, 77-James Russell, Student Manager-Richard Powell; second row, Coach Jerry Shaffer, Coach Rick Page, 64-Bo Keller, 34-Mike Taylor, 42-Chris Gray, 87-Mike Marshall, Coach Dick Matkin, Coach Ken Ard; third row, 88-Chris Winters, 83-Troy Ripple, 78-James Wright, 46-Dan Whitt, 37-Randy Cox, 99-Danny Leopard, 74-Brad McDonald, 52-Tim Pelton; fourth row, 25-Wayne Tyson, 49-Doug Gollahon, 65-Jimmy Hughes, 24-Robert Martinez, 35-Tony Garner, Bret Burleson, 85-Roy Fuentes, 20-Dale Morgan, 81-Grant Thomason; fifth row, 61-Jim Chaney, 79-Paul Adams, 17-Roy McClendon, 24-Rickey Blackman, 50-Kevin Adams, 58-Bob Skipwith, 48-Bruce Cryer, 75-Mike Helm, 80-Jack Hirmon; top row, 66-Lon Wallace, 10-Rock King, 18-Mark Whitehead, 67-Russell E. Jones, 60-Phil Lemons, 70-Gary Taylor, 84-Garth Touchstone, 55-Jess Croley, 63-Danny Schultz, 9-Ronnie Cross. (Photo courtesy of Jerry Shaffer)

Contents

Prologue xiii
Introduction xv
History Of the Wylie Pirates Prior to 1977 1
The Players 11
The Coaches 25
Game One, Wylie vs. Diamond Hill 30
Game Two, Wylie vs. Kaufman 34
Game Three, Wylie vs. Farmersville 38
Game Four, Wylie vs. Justin Northwest 44
Game Five, Wylie vs. Cedar Hill 46
Game Six, Wylie vs. Midlothian 48
Game Seven, Wylie vs. Allen 51
Game Eight, Wylie vs. Red Oak 54
Game Nine, Wylie vs. Forney 56
Game Ten, Wylie vs. Ferris 84
Bi-district Playoff, Wylie vs. Granbury 87
Regional Playoff, Wylie vs. Breckenridge 93
State Quarterfinal Playoff, Wylie vs. Mount Vernon 107
State Semifinal Playoff, Wylie vs. Childress 113

State Championship, Wylie vs. Bellville....................... 118
Postseason Awards.. 132
Their Place In History....................................... 136
The Legend Of AHMO... 140
The Years Since.. 144
The 1977 Wylie Pirates....................................... 157
Wylie Pirates 1977 Game Results 159
Playoff game capsules.. 161
Index.. 165

Acknowledgement

The facts on which this work is based were obtained from interviews conducted by the author (most of which were recorded on tape), game films and newspaper articles from the day. The work is accurate to the best of the author's knowledge.

Prologue

You won't find AHMO in any dictionary. It means pride, determination, stamina, courage, sportsmanship and fair play. It means teamwork, true grit, gung ho and giving it your all.
    In Wylie, Texas, it means everything.

Introduction

Small towns are often called "sleepy."

The small town of Wylie, Texas, is an exception to that rule.

Since the 1940s, Wylie has been referred to as "Wide Awake Wylie," so nicknamed because of its citizens' penchant for staying out late on the town in that decade.

Today, Wylie is no longer the "small town" it once was. Close to 25,000 people populate Wylie. New businesses are constantly being welcomed in, new homes are being built and new schools are opening. As more and more people look to get away from the big city, the population of Wylie continues to increase. Located immediately south of Lake Lavon in south central Collin County about 30 miles to the northeast of Downtown Dallas and about 10 miles east of the booming suburb of Plano, Wylie has become a popular place to move in recent years for people who want to live close to the big city, but still keep their distance.

In the late 1970s, Wylie certainly appeared sleepy on the surface. It had a population of less than 4,000 and featured only three restaurants. At that time, the town was probably known best for the Ladylike Shop—a four-building shopping center in the heart of Downtown Wylie at which patrons could buy coats and skiing equipment. The store was immensely popular, drawing shoppers from all over Texas (despite the scarcity of snow and skiing weather) and other states. The Ladylike Shop remained a popular attraction in Wylie until it was destroyed by fire in 1998.

The city of Wylie has always lived up to its "Wide Awake" moniker with its lively population that epitomizes the term, "Southern Hospitality." The people of Wylie have always been a close-knit group. This became apparent by the way they rallied to rebuild their town following a devastating tornado in 1993 and several downtown fires in 1998. Wylie-ites stick together no matter what the hardship.

They are particularly loyal to their high school football team. In Texas, nothing brings people together like football—especially in a small town with only one high school. A catchphrase made popular on Friday nights by the people of Wylie during the football playoffs in the late 1970s— "Last one to leave town, turn out the lights"—says it all about that town's loyalty as far as attendance at high school football games and support of the team in general. Game days were always eventful.

"People would decorate the streets," said Macklyn Stripling, who began a long career as an English and art teacher at Wylie High School in the fall of 1977. "The parents would get out and paint the streets, especially when we played Allen, because that was our biggest rival. That's what made it fun. I'm from Lubbock, and my high school was about 10 times bigger than Wylie. That was a neat bit of small town that I had never experienced before."

In 1977, the Wylie Pirates rewarded the town with a 13-2 record and the school's first state football championship.

That state title did not come easy. Once the playoffs started, the Pirates were decided underdogs in most of the games. It took two last-gasp, miracle wins in the playoffs to advance. Then, in the championship game, it took knocking off the No. 1 team in the state at that level.

If that weren't enough, Wylie almost turned the trick again in 1978 despite graduating many of the key players from the championship team. And they would have won back-to-back state titles if not for a career performance by running back from Sealy High School in the 1978 championship game (that running back wound up in the NFL Hall of Fame).

A loss in that contest, however, could not tarnish what the Wylie Pirate football team had accomplished over the previous two seasons. They had given their fans their money's worth and more.

This is the story of the Wylie Pirates' 1977 state championship season as seen through the eyes of the players and coaches who lived it—told in their own words from the opening kickoff in September against Fort Worth Diamond Hill until the final seconds ticked away in the state championship game against Bellville more than three months later.

But it is also much more.

It is the story of a group of young men uniting for a common cause and beating the odds to reach the summit. It is the story of the thrill of victory that few high school football players get to experience. It is the story of heart, determination and of dreams coming true—not just for a football team, but also for an entire town.

"All of us were like family," said Jess Croley, one of the players on that state championship team. "It took not only the team and the parents, but it took the whole community to do that."

History Of the Wylie Pirates Prior to 1977

The story of Wylie's 1977 football championship season actually began three years earlier with the hiring of Jerry G. Shaffer as head football coach and athletic director of Wylie High School in the Wylie Independent School District.

Prior to Coach Shaffer's arrival in 1974, the Pirates had their loyal fan base, but had not achieved any postseason success to speak of in their long history. In fact, Wylie made the playoffs only twice in the school's 73-year history before Shaffer came on board.

The first time the Wylie Pirates tasted the postseason was in 1941. At that time, the University Interscholastic League (UIL)—the governing body of the major high school sports in Texas—classified schools as (in order of largest enrollment to smallest) 2A, A, B, or six-man. In the postseason, schools played only other schools in the same classification. That year, 2A was the only class to play to a state championship; Class A played two postseason rounds and Class B played one round.

The 1941 Pirates won their district and squared off against Bells in a Class B bi-district playoff game. The Pirates knew this game was their one shot at glory, since no more playoff games would follow that year. But they fell just short, losing to Bells by a 7-6 score.

Senior quarterback Truman Seabourn scored Wylie's only touchdown in that game against Bells. To get an idea of how many people attended Wylie High School in those days, consider that Truman and 15 other people made up the WHS Class of 1942.

The Wylie Pirates faithful had no idea that 30 years would pass by before their team would sniff the postseason again. But no matter how bad things got—and at times, they got bad—the fans stuck to their beloved maroon and white like glue, much the same way Boston Red Sox, Chicago White Sox and Chicago Cubs fans stay with their teams in baseball and Cleveland Browns fans do in football.

One of those fans who has stuck with the Pirates through thick and thin is Kenneth Nall, who played quarterback for Wylie High School in 1961–62 and was once presented with a plaque by the WHS administrative staff for attending every varsity football game (home and away) over a 25-year period. It took a heart attack, literally, to break Kenneth's consecutive Wylie football game attendance streak in 1991. As soon as he recovered, he was back in the stands, cheering on the Pirates.

In the 1950s and 1960s, the Wylie Pirate football teams and their fans knew that the school had no playoff history to speak of, yet they were almost oblivious to the postseason drought. Friday nights during September, October and early November meant high school football in Wylie, period, and people attended the games and cheered on the Pirates no matter what without thinking of past struggles or failures. It was just a tradition for the small town of Wylie, according to Kenneth Nall, to attend high school football games on Friday nights.

"I'll stick by this all the time," Kenneth said emphatically. "Even when I played—even when we didn't win a game when I was a sophomore (fall of 1960)—Wylie people will come to the games. I don't know why, they just never did give up on you. The town just backed it, and still will."

The Pirates were had their share of athletes from the 1940s on through the 1970s. In the 1940s, players such as Bobby Click, Billy Sasse and Truman Seabourn starred on the gridiron for Wylie. In the mid 1950s, it was James Cross, Winston Watkins and Wally Watkins leading the way, followed by the Clemmons brothers, Russell and Wayne, at the end of that decade. The 1960s saw the Pirates field such football standouts as Kenneth Nall, Mike Hale, Red Benson, Joey Schiefer, Richard Parker, John Housewright and Truman Tackett.

At times in the 1950s under Coach R.C. Dodd and in 1960s under Coach Grady Burnett, the Pirates put together a few solid seasons but were unable to take home that elusive district championship trophy. In 1968, they finished 7-3 under Coach Burnett but did not make the playoffs (prior to 1982, only the champion of each district in Texas qualified for the postseason under the UIL's playoff format). In 1970 under Coach Charles Birdsong, the Pirates ended the season at 9-1 and did not qualify for postseason play. Their one loss was to Farmersville, which represented the district in the playoffs. At the time, the Pirates played in District 13 of Class A, with 4A being the highest after the UIL revamped its playoff format in 1951.

Finally, in 1971, the Pirates posted a 9-0-1 record and won the District 13-A championship for the first time in three decades, led by Ronnie Rowell, Charlie Parker (Richard's younger brother), Ken Christopher and David Green. In 10 regular season games, the Pirates outscored their opponents, 359-15, with an astounding eight shutouts. Their one tie was a 0-0 affair against their old rival, Farmersville, which finished tied for first in the district with Wylie; the Pirates represented the district in the postseason based on having the most offensive penetrations inside the opponent's 20 yard line against Farmersville.

By 1971, much had changed in the 30 years since the Pirates had last won district. This time, there was a state title at stake, and the Pirates threw down the gauntlet with a 38-6 thrashing of Van Alstyne in the bi-district (opening) round of the playoffs.

In the second round, however, Crowley did a number on the Pirates for the regional championship by using running back Jackie Baylor to repeatedly run a play known as the "belly series." This play was virtually the same thing as the option play favored by so many high school football teams in Texas throughout the 1980s and 1990s, and to some extent, the early 2000s. Crowley blanked Wylie in that game, 30-0, to send the Pirates home for the winter.

And the Pirate fans would have to wait once more.

Change was in the air for Wylie in 1972. Head coach Charles Birdsong, who had taken over the program two years earlier when Grady Burnett became principal of Wylie High School, departed and was replaced by Gerald Lloyd. Increased enrollment necessitated a move up to Class 2A for the Pirates. The team's two big stars, tailback Ronnie Rowell and quarterback Charlie Parker, graduated in the spring of 1972. Little did the team and its fans know that a couple of long, arduous years on the football field lay ahead.

The Pirates followed that 1971 bi-district championship season by losing the first nine games of the 1972 campaign. In those nine losses, Wylie scored a total of 26 points—an average of less than three points per game. At one point in the season, they were shut out four times in a row. Somehow, they scratched out a 16-8 win over Grand Saline in the final game of the season.

It appeared things could not get much worse for the Pirates, but amazingly, they did. In 1973, Wylie finished 0-10, giving them a 1-19 mark to that point under Coach Lloyd. In those two years combined, the Pirates scored 107 points over 20 games for an average of just over five points per contest.

"None of that was really Gerald's fault," Coach Shaffer explained. "I still have most all the film of those two years. The kids played pretty good and pretty hard, the best I can tell. They just were outmanned…they moved up a classification and were in a very competitive district with Rockwall, Kaufman, some of those people. And they played pretty close games. They didn't get blown out much."

Benji Gibson, a 1974 graduate of Wylie High School, played most of the downs at quarterback for the Pirates during those two years under Coach Lloyd. Benji loved to throw the ball and was good at it; as a freshman on the Pirates' junior varsity team when Coach Birdsong was still at Wylie, Benji averaged three touchdown passes a game. By the time Benji reached the Pirate varsity team, Coach Lloyd had taken over and instituted the option for the Wylie offense. The results were a far cry from what the Pirates had hoped they would be.

"We went to the option, and apparently I was not an option quarterback, because we couldn't score points," Benji said. "I was more suited for throwing the ball."

Though the Pirates fought hard and played close games in those two years under Coach Lloyd, 1-19 was 1-19, and Coach Shaffer was hired to replace him in 1974.

Coach Shaffer came to Wylie as a winner. At age 23, he had been an offensive assistant for nearby Rockwall High School when that team won the Class 2A state championship in 1963. His other coaching stops included Texas high schools Kilgore, Duncanville and Sherman before he landed in Wylie.

Shaffer was an offensive-minded coach who implemented in Wylie an offense that started with head coach Bill Yeoman at the University of Houston in the mid-1960s, the veer offense. When Rockwall won state in 1963 with Coach Shaffer calling the plays, the offense ran mostly in a variation of several different wing-T formations used by colleges in the pre-veer days.

The veer offense, which was a variation of the wishbone offense made famous by the University of Texas in the 1960s, gave the Pirates three options to run the ball, depending on what the defensive linemen did. In a nutshell, the veer offense was a series of reads; the quarterback would read the defense and determine to which back he would give the ball or if he would keep it himself. The word "veer" was derived from the path the back took to the outside.

Teams could also pass the ball using the veer offense using a series of play-action fakes if the quarterback liked what he saw downfield after he read the defense. Under Coach Shaffer in the mid and late 1970s (and throughout the 80s as well), Wylie utilized this option of the veer offense often.

The new head coach, still young at 33 when he arrived in Wylie, assembled an even younger staff of assistant coaches. Nearly all of Shaffer's assistants on the high school staff were in their 20s. But they were all hungry. And they all knew their football.

The veer offense was an instant success in Wylie. The Pirates showed immediate improvement under Coach Shaffer.

In their first game of the 1974 season, the Pirates pounded Van Alstyne, 34-6. They followed that with a 12-0 blanking of Frisco and a 14-2 win over Farmersville, and before they knew it, they were 3-0 and had tripled the number of wins they had registered in the two previous years combined.

But the Pirates won just two of their next six games to take a 5-4 record into the season finale against Forney. What resulted in that finale was one of the landmark games in Wylie football history, according to Coach Shaffer.

On November 15, 1974, the Pirates traveled to Forney to take on the Jackrabbits in the final game in Forney's stadium. The Jackrabbits were set to begin play in a new facility in 1975.

At the time, Forney sported an 8-1 record and was competing for the district title. They needed a win in the last game of the season against Wylie to stay in the race. The Pirates had nothing to play for but pride, though they knew with a win they could clinch a winning season.

The men in maroon and white stopped the Jackrabbits short, stunning them, 15-6, on that cold mid-November night to knock them out of the running for the district title and give Wylie a 6-4 record on the season. Danny Meek scored both of Wylie's touchdowns, one on a 40-yard pass from Jeff Ammerman in the first quarter and one on a two-yard run in the third period. Danny's third quarter TD made it 13-6, and on a fake, Gary Foster's pass found Trent Thomason in the end zone for the two-point conversion to put Wylie up by nine at 15-6.

The Wylie defense held strong against Forney, led by Bill King, Tom Burris, Danny Meek and Jeff Ammerman, who was playing his first game of the season at the cornerback position. He came up with a big interception to stop a Forney drive near the end of the game. Darrell Wright recovered a fumble early to set up Wylie's first touchdown.

"These kids we had in '74 were really a gritty bunch of kids," Coach Shaffer remembered. "They were ready to play in that last game...(Forney) scored first, on their field...you could just see how you could just check it in so easily. But they just kind of decided they weren't going to lose. The kids played extraordinarily well, we had a couple of little wrinkles in our plan that they executed exceptionally well, and we beat those suckers."

One picture in the 1975 Wylie High School annual says it all—the image of Coach Shaffer and Coach Rick Page, Wylie's defensive coordinator, congratulating each other with wide smiles after that win over Forney. Both coaches have pointed to that photograph as a personal favorite.

The Pirates finished 1974 with a 6-4 record. Though they did not make the playoffs, they had posted a winning record for the first time in three years and had improved over the previous two years by leaps and bounds.

"That gave us a winning record, and we were trying to make a change and get things going," Coach Page recalled. "We really had things going our way. We won a lot of games that people didn't think we needed to, but we really hadn't beaten anybody that was really good yet (before Forney). The last game of the year, we were playing Forney, and they still had a chance to get into the district championship. They were a huge favorite over us, an established program. We were fortunate enough to beat them there at the end. It was just a signal to the kids, to the young people that were coming up and going to be part of the program in the future that it was different…that Wylie could now compete with the big dogs. It just made a big, big difference in the whole outlook of the team, the community and everything."

One of the obstacles Coach Shaffer and his staff and players constantly battled in 1974 was the worn down facilities in Wylie. It was clear the stadium, the field house and the high school had long since passed their useful days—particularly the high school. The building that is now Harrison Intermediate School housed grades seven through 12, but there were not enough classrooms to accommodate all the students. To compensate for a lack of space, the school district used some old classrooms in a building located just down a gravel road where Hartman Elementary School now sits.

Despite these conditions, there was a light at the end of the tunnel. Just before Coach Shaffer's arrival in 1974, the Wylie Independent School District passed a bond referendum to build a new high school, stadium and field house to replace the outdated facilities. The school district was not willing to put money into improving the old facilities because they had been anticipating building new ones for some time.

"We inherited about as bad a facility as you could get," Coach Shaffer remembered. "But it wasn't all bad because everything that happened was an improvement. There was some looking forward and some anticipation of improving…it was a time for change. Change was going to happen whether I was here or not. They were probably going to improve considerably, and I was fortunate enough to be here at that juncture."

Wylie was still one of the smaller schools, enrollment-wise, in Class 2A in 1974, having just moved up from Class A two years earlier. One of the problems Coach Shaffer had to deal with his first couple of years in Wylie was the low student turnout for participation in the football program; a lack of on-field success in the two years before his arrival may have deterred some kids from playing that otherwise would have participated.

In 1975, the Pirates followed their 6-4 season with a 4-5-1 performance. The tie was against Van Alstyne in the opener, 0-0. Forney exacted revenge on the Pirates by defeating them in the last game of the season in the final game at the old Pirate Stadium—just as the Pirates had done with Forney in 1974 in the last game at Forney's old stadium.

In 1976, the Pirates finally welcomed a new stadium to replace their worn-down venue. The new stadium was supposed to have been ready for the 1975 season, but excessive rain in the summer of 1975 prevented its completion. With the new stadium (which was built next to the new high school) came a new field house and workout facility for the athletes of Wylie High School.

The Pirates kicked off the 1976 season with three consecutive games at their new home field, which was christened Pirate Stadium. They lost the first two contests to Rockwall (by the score of 13-6) and Kaufman (by a 14-8 count). While it was clear the Pirate defense was performing, the offense was off to a slow start. Junior fullback Wayne Tyson scored the only touchdown for Wylie in both games.

The third time was a charm for the 1976 Pirates. They beat Farmersville, 7-0, in week three for their first win at new Pirate Stadium (again, Wayne scored the only touchdown for the Pirates). In the days when Plano, McKinney and Frisco were all one-high school towns, the Wylie-Farmersville grudge match stood as one of Collin County's oldest and fiercest rivalries, though they did not compete in the same district for most of the 1970s and 1980s.

A 9-6 loss in week four to Justin Northwest, however, put Coach Shaffer's team at 1-3 in their first four games of 1976. To say the least, things did not look promising. The silver lining of losing three out of the first four games was that they were all non-district games and did not count in the standings.

The Pirates typically ran a symmetrical offense, with a tight end on each end, which did not require them to "flip-flop" personnel on the offensive line. In the first four games, Coach Shaffer and his staff experimented with a different offense that included an automatic split end and an automatic tight end. Since the offense to the tight end side and the offense to the split end side were completely different, this required the team to flip-flop personnel to make the plays work. Unfortunately, the Pirates were unable to successfully run the new offense in the first four games of the 1976 season.

"That hurt us those first four games," Coach Shaffer recalled. "We didn't play as well. Technically, we weren't as good because of a poor decision on my part."

After the Pirates scrapped their offensive experiment, an amazing thing happened. Led by senior quarterback Gary Foster, the Pirates rallied for six consecutive wins, all district games, and finished undefeated in District 12-2A play at 6-0. For the first time in five years, the Pirates were district champions; they had finished their first year in new Pirate Stadium with a 7-3 regular season mark and won the third district crown in school history.

Wylie clinched the District 12-2A title with a win over Forney—in the Jackrabbits' brand new stadium—in the second-to-last game of the regular season. Long after the game ended on that early November evening in 1976, Coach Shaffer recalled that it began to snow, a rare occurrence in northeast Texas. This was a significant night for Coach Shaffer, as well as for most people in Wylie, for it was the day that former Pirates head football and basketball coach and longtime Wylie civic leader R.C. Dodd passed away at the young age of 51.

"That was a real personal loss for me," Coach Shaffer remembered, "because I had a lot of appreciation for R.C."

Two weeks later, the Pirates hammered Granbury, 33-14, in the opening round of the playoffs to win the bi-district championship at nearby Garland Memorial Stadium (now Homer B. Johnson Stadium). That playoff game against Granbury marked the first time Wylie had ever played football on artificial turf.

Bowie provided the next obstacle in the regional championship, and they turned the tables on Wylie, winning, 53-14, at Fouts Field in Denton. The Pirates were eliminated in the regional game by a lopsided margin just as they had been five years earlier against Crowley. Some of the players and coaches from that Wylie team refer to the Bowie playoff game as "the massacre."

One of the things to which Coach Shaffer attributed that one-sided score was a sharp decline in temperature at halftime for which the Pirates were simply not prepared. A bitterly cold wind started blowing. The Pirates began the game in their short sleeves on that sultry mid-November night and did not anticipate needing any cold weather gear, therefore they brought none with them that night. Whereas the temperature was in the 60s when the game started, it was in the 30s when the game ended. That, combined with the pre-game sweat the Pirates had worked up, made for an "unbelievably bad scene," according to Coach Shaffer.

"That Bowie game where we got knocked out of the playoffs…up to that point, that was the most physical game I had been involved in," said cornerback Roy Fuentes, who was a junior in the fall of 1976. "We were so cold. We couldn't keep warm at all. We were totally unprepared for that (change in the weather). Aside from Bowie being an excellent team, we had to combat the weather as well. It was a double whammy."

Coach Shaffer agreed. "We played Bowie, and we played the weather, and I'm telling you, our kids about froze to death. They were on the sidelines just shivering. And the coaches, too...that was significant thing from a coaching point of view because we never let that occur again. To let that occur, that was really a serious oversight on my part.

"I have to say, I was so proud of our kids. We rarely played below what our capability was, and that was one time I think we did. But I don't blame the kids. If we'd been prepared for (the change in weather), we probably would have gotten beaten, but nothing like what we did."

As promised, the Pirates were always prepared for the weather from that point on with Coach Shaffer at the helm. This preparedness would come into play the following year during a playoff game on a frigid night against Childress in Wichita Falls.

One of the good things that came out of the loss to Bowie was near the end of the game, with the outcome having long since been decided. At that time, Coach Shaffer began to insert several backups who went on to play a major role the following year on the state championship team.

"We had our butts kicked at halftime," said Tony Garner, who was a junior flanker/strong safety for the Pirates in 1976. "When that cold came in, that just did us in...until the last three or four minutes. I'm sure (Bowie) had their scrubs in, but basically the team that won state the following year, (Shaffer) put all of us in. We ended up coming down and putting in two touchdowns in the last three minutes of the game."

Though the 1976 season ended early, people were starting to take notice. The boys came up with a six-game winning streak when it counted most and brought the district championship trophy back to Wylie. Things were really beginning to click for the Pirates.

"I think the whole program at that point realized, both the coaches and kids, understood what it took to win," said Rock King, who was a freshman punter and place-kicker on that 1976 team. "I think all the younger kids that were exposed to those other kids, it was a benefit to all of us to be able to play with them and practice with them and to have that kind of success and watch them succeed...I think about half the game is psychological, anyway. When you believe that you can achieve those things, that helps."

Before the 1977 season started, the papers finally gave Wylie some respect. The Associated Press preseason rankings listed Wylie as the 9th best Class 2A team in Texas—the first time the AP had ever ranked Wylie in its football poll. The Pirates were a preseason favorite to repeat as champion of District 12-2A.

"We knew that the program was on the upswing, and that we were in hopes that after a year of off-season that we would be a little bit better physically than we had been the year before," said Bruce King, who coached Wylie's secondary and receivers in the mid-1970s, "but of course, that doesn't always translate to wins and losses and that sort of thing. But we felt like we had a chance to be a little bit better (than in 1976)."

But Coach Shaffer's expectations of the Pirates for 1977 were not based on newspaper polls or rankings.

"He went to great lengths to ensure that we paid no attention (to polls)," said Bob Skipwith, who played center for the 1977 Pirates. "He would downplay everything… 'Polls mean nothing to us,' 'You've got to win it on the field,' 'If you guys spend too much time reading your news clippings, then you're not focused on the right things.'"

Though the local newspapers were taking notice of Wylie, no one had yet declared the 1977 Pirates as "the team on the brink," so to speak, simply because of a lack of a winning history if nothing else.

"It felt like certainly we should win district again, but not much else," said defensive tackle Chuck Edge, who was a sophomore on that bi-district champion team of 1976. "Since Wylie had never been that far, we'd never thought about it. You go two games deep and you think, 'Wow, that's great!' You never really fathom going 15, 16 games and actually winning (the state title). There were no great expectations."

Not at first, anyway.

The Players

In 1977, the Pirates returned many of the key players from that bi-district champion team of the year before, with two notable exceptions.

Quarterback Gary Foster, an athletic student who lettered in nearly every sport at Wylie, graduated in the spring of 1977. He had been a starter on the varsity football team at Wylie since his sophomore year (at free safety) in the fall of 1974, Coach Shaffer's first year in Wylie. Gary's departure left a great void in the Pirates' football team as far as athleticism and leadership.

"Gary was a great leader," said Ronnie Cross, who was a junior on the 1976 Pirates team and a longtime friend of Gary's. "He just had a knack about him. He was one of those guys that it didn't matter where you had him on the field, he was gonna win. That was his mindset.

"It was like a 'follow me' kind of deal. He would show you the way. He demanded a lot in the huddles from his folks to step up and get it done, and they always responded, because he was going to get it done. That's just the way Gary is. He's a super competitor and a big winner, and he's been that way his whole life. It didn't matter what sport he was playing."

For an entire day, the Wylie coaching staff gathered at Coach Shaffer's house pondered over a solution to the dilemma as to who would replace Gary Foster at quarterback. At the end of the day, they were left with two choices.

One of those was senior Ronnie Cross, who was a gifted but unproven commodity. Ronnie had backed up Gary under center on the 1976 team and had not played much, but played enough to letter. Besides being the second-string signal caller, Ronnie played sporadically at strong safety as a junior.

Ronnie, like Gary Foster, was not built like the prototypical quarterback—he stood at 5-foot-10 and weighed 145 pounds. He was not the fastest kid on the block. But athleticism ran in Ronnie's family—his father, James Cross, had been a four-year letterman for the Wylie Pirates as a punter nearly a quarter century earlier while playing on the same Pirates team as Benji Gibson's father, Jesse "Sonny" Gibson. Ronnie's teammates tagged him with the nickname "Blood," and although no one remembers exactly why, it is believed that his red hair had something to do with it.

Despite lacking the size and speed that the prototypical quarterback possessed, Ronnie had two things going for him—he had a rifle for a right arm and he wanted to win. A true competitor, Ronnie suffered a broken tailbone in practice during the first week of two-a-days in 1977, and that slowed him somewhat. But he was determined to play his senior year, and the injury did not keep him down long.

"He was the quarterback from pee wee football on up," said Phil Lemons, Ronnie's cousin, who played left offensive tackle for the 1977 Pirates and also grew up living next door to Ronnie. "He always played that position. He was a real good athlete. He could throw the ball. He was a really good baseball player. He didn't have the size, but he had a lot of athletic ability. He just never would give up. If he wanted something, he just kept trying until he got it."

The other choice for quarterback arrived a year earlier, in the summer of 1976, when Roger "Rock" King transferred from Beeville to Wylie for his freshman year. Before Rock was two years old, his brother, Bruce—10 years his senior—was calling him Rockhead, Rock revealed, "because of the size of my head and the hardness of it, I guess. Thankfully, they shortened it to Rock, and it stuck."

Rock had attended junior high in three different places in Texas—Beeville, Crowley and Burleson—and he played some tight end on junior high football teams. Rock could throw the ball as well, but a dislocated left shoulder suffered during two-a-days in 1976 prevented him from playing quarterback for the Pirates as a freshman (though he threw right-handed). Doctors told Rock his shoulder needed surgery, but he decided to wait until after the football season. In the meantime, the Pirates would take advantage of Rock's strong leg by using him as a punter and place-kicker for the varsity team. He also played sparingly at linebacker for the Pirates in his first year in Wylie.

In 1977 as a sophomore (though he was a year older than all the kids in his class, having been held back in the seventh grade), Rock was being considered to fill the vacant quarterback position after his shoulder surgery.

Rock's path to Wylie was paved by a series of fates. In 1975, one of Coach Shaffer's assistants, Hardee McCrary, was leaving Wylie and suggested that they hire his college friend, Bruce King, as the Pirates' head baseball coach and defensive secondary/offensive receivers coach to replace him. A couple of years earlier, Bruce and Hardee had graduated from Austin College in Sherman, which was Coach Shaffer's alma mater (Hardee's later coaching stops included Southern Methodist, Tulane, Rice and the University of Texas).

A year later in 1976, when Coach Ken Ard was promoted to the high school football team from the junior high school, it left an opening; Bruce suggested that his father, John, would fit the bill.

John King was still relatively new to coaching, and he was offered a coaching job at Wylie Junior High in the summer of 1976. It was a little different coaching job than what he was doing at the time—John was the head baseball coach and an assistant football coach in Texas at the Class 4A high school level (4A became 5A in 1980). But since he wanted to get Rock involved in a quality high school football program, he accepted Coach Shaffer's offer, and the King family relocated to Wylie.

"It was a sacrifice, career-wise, for him, to come to Wylie and go back to work at the junior high," Rock explained. "Looking back at it now, I think he probably did what was best for me."

John King coached in the Wylie ISD for one year before accepting a coaching job at a junior high school in nearby Plano before the 1977 school year, and Rock continued to attend Wylie High School. One of the deciding factors in John King's decision to leave the WISD after only one year was the fact that his duties as a coach in Plano did not include scouting, whereas in Wylie he did have to scout the upcoming opponents every Friday night. Since he did not scout as a coach in Plano, John's Friday nights were free to watch Rock play.

Coach Shaffer was expecting to get only a junior high football coach out of the deal, but he ended up getting much more than he could have imagined with the addition of Rock to his team.

The other departure from the team was unexpected. Senior tight end/outside linebacker David Leopard, an all-district player on offense and defense in 1976, walked off the field during two-a-days before the 1977 season started, according to Coach Shaffer and several of the players. Many members of the Pirates have said that David was being courted by Division I universities to play football and had actually received letters from those schools. It was not common at that time for Division I universities to recruit from the schools in the smaller classifications in Texas, which shows just how good a player David was.

Jess Croley, a senior offensive tackle/defensive end on that Wylie team and a friend of David's, said simply of David's football ability, "He was awesome."

As per the coach's policy, David's gear hung in his locker for a few days should he decide to return to the team. But he did not, and the uniform was taken up and the locker cleaned out. Once that happened, the uniform was not reissued to the same player during the same season, a rule from which Coach Shaffer never varied during his 14-year tenure at Wylie.

"That was a real sad thing, for me and for him," Coach Shaffer lamented of David Leopard's departure from the team. "Football was real important to him. It makes my heart ache even right now to think about that incident."

"David probably could have went (to college) just about anywhere. He was tall, he was fast and he had great hands," said Tony Garner, a senior in 1977 who grew up on the same street as David. "He just got mixed up in the wrong group. The issue was, he had been at practice/not at practice. He was a huge asset when he was on the field.

"(David's departure) was kind of twofold. We were all kind of sad to see him go, and the other side was it was a conflict that was now gone. We all hated to see him go because we'd known him forever. We didn't want him to leave the team, but it had been such an issue and the friction was there."

Later in the season, Coach Shaffer brought up David's younger brother, Danny, to the varsity team for the Pirates' playoff run. Danny played a key role on the Pirates' state-runner up team the following year as a running back.

But David never played another down for the Pirates after leaving practice that day before the 1977 season started. Running back Wayne Mayberry, who like David Leopard was a senior that year, said of David, "He would have had a college scholarship paid for. He just couldn't stand to have anybody telling him what to do…that was a big loss. We all hated to see him give it up like that, but we also couldn't dwell on it. We hated to see him leave, but they'll put somebody else in your spot if you don't want to play."

One of their star two-way players was gone, but as Wayne indicated, the Pirates went searching elsewhere for a replacement. They found their new tight end in the form of a move-in from the Burleson area named Doug Gollahon. Doug was a longtime friend of Rock King's—they had grown up together in Burleson—and he took much the same path to Wylie that Rock did. In fact, John King, Rock's father, and Roy Gollahon, Doug's father, were good friends who had both gotten into coaching as a second career; when John vacated his coaching position at Wylie Junior High in the summer of 1977, he suggested that Roy would make a great fit to coach at WJHS. Coach Shaffer hired Roy Gollahon as a football coach at Wylie Junior High in the summer of 1977, and the Gollahon family moved from Burleson to Wylie.

"With my dad leaving, he knew that Roy was looking for an opportunity to go to work and coach," Rock explained, then added with a smile, "Of course, he knew that Doug would come along with the package."

Ironically, Doug had attended one of the Wylie football playoff games in 1976 to watch Rock play. At the time, Doug had no idea his family would be moving to Wylie in just a few short months.

"From Rock, I knew they had a pretty good athletic program, and I went and watched 'em play, and they had a pretty good ballclub," Doug said.

The Wylie coaching staff did not know immediately what they had with Doug, who was nicknamed "Fudgie" by his Pirate teammates. When he came to Wylie for his senior year, he was primarily a baseball player. He did not play football in Burleson his sophomore or junior years because of operations on both of his elbows. He had already made up his mind he was going to play football his senior year, and in fact, he had been through spring training for football as a junior while still in Burleson.

In Wylie, the fact that Doug was going to play on the same team with Rock, who was his best friend growing up in Burleson, made it that much more exciting for both of them. The two had played on several sports teams, including baseball and basketball, together growing up.

When Doug came to Wylie, he did not know what position he was going to play; it was decided that he would play tight end, since that was the position he played as a freshman in Burleson (he had been a quarterback in junior high). He worked out all summer with the Pirates in 1977 and had thrown the ball around with Rock quite a bit. Still, Doug was not considered to start at tight end until David Leopard left the team, and even then, it was a couple of games into the season before Doug became a starter. But once he did, there was no stopping him.

Everyone recognized that Doug had a gift—when passes were thrown his way, the ball stuck to his hands like glue. In fact, in newspaper accounts of the Wylie football games in 1977, Doug was often referred to as "glue-fingered."

"I think it's an attitude," Doug explained. "I firmly believe that if you're a receiver, if you touch the ball, you should catch it. I believe that with all my heart."

Receivers coach Bruce King said of his tight end, "We knew Doug was a really good kid and a good athlete…His athleticism really lay in his ability to just catch a ball if it got close to him. He didn't have extraordinary size or speed at all, but he understood the offense and what we were trying to do. We didn't even know when he came in what position he would play, but he just fit into the thing so well, and because of the way our offense evolved over the year, it was a magical fit for us."

Doug was athletic and had good hand-eye coordination, and though he was not big for a tight end (5-10, 165 pounds), his excellent coordination allowed him to effectively do the type of blocking that was needed to run the veer offense, or "shadow blocking," as Coach Shaffer called it. A shadow blocker was required to get in the cornerback's way and drive him off the line of scrimmage.

Doug was already familiar with Rock's style of throwing, and it did not take him long to adapt to Ronnie's. The addition of Doug Gollahon to the team turned out to be huge, and he helped to provide many offensive fireworks throughout the 1977 season with both quarterbacks.

Before the season, it was decided that Garth Touchstone, a tall junior who played tight end on offense, would fill the middle linebacker position. At 184 pounds, Garth was one of the bigger guys on the team and was a great fit at tight end. The coaches conceded late in the season that Garth was probably playing out of position at middle linebacker, though he did have some shining moments at the position in 1977.

"Touchstone was not your typical middle linebacker," strong safety Tony Garner said. "He was probably more of an offensive player. I don't know how many passes he caught, but I would suspect he had a huge number."

The 1977 Wylie Pirates were not the quickest team around, and they certainly were not the largest. In fact, Coach Shaffer called them the "smallest, slowest team that's ever won a state championship in the state of Texas at that classification (2A). I'm extremely confident in that."

Size was an advantage for Wylie at few, if any, positions. Only two players on the roster—senior offensive tackle Paul Adams and senior defensive end/offensive tackle Jess Croley, were listed at more than 200 pounds (Paul tipped the scale at 200 and Jess weighed a cool 201). Jess actually weighed less than that; upon his graduation a few months after football season, he weighed about 189. Jess and Paul made up a combination that alternated every other series at right offensive tackle for the majority of the season.

In addition to being small, this group of Pirates was not likely to win any speed races. They had a few players that could break 11 seconds in the 100 yard dash, but none that could run it in faster than 10 seconds. In fact, in the spring of 1978, the Pirates' track team—with many of the same players that helped win the football state championship in the fall of 1977—finished dead last at the district track meet, albeit by only two-thirds of a point.

Bob Skipwith, who played center for the Pirates, remarked, "We all knew, especially in the playoffs, that we were the underdogs and we were totally outmanned in probably every facet. The line, the speed of the receivers, the speed and quickness of the backs…it was a struggle every time we took the field, and we all knew it, and we sort of sucked it up and tried to do what we could do to try to win."

Though they were not fast individually, the Pirates had good team speed off the ball, especially on the offensive line. They could execute and they had great technique. "You hardly ever saw them get knocked off their feet," Coach Shaffer said. "They were just extraordinarily nimble and agile."

What the Pirates lacked in size and speed they made up for with experience and smarts. Names like Collins, Mayberry, Wallace, Garner, Fuentes, Skipwith, Schultz, Morgan, Lemons, Croley and Tyson—just to name a few—were battle-tested veterans of the high-school gridiron, having played extensively for Wylie on the district champion 1976 team.

The offensive line, though not large or particularly fast, was one to be reckoned with. Chuck Edge at left guard, Phil Lemons at left tackle, Bob Skipwith at center, Jess Croley at right tackle and Lon Wallace at right guard represented the Pirate starting five on the O-line, and though they averaged only about 175 pounds per man (as far as listed weight), this was an intelligent, tough, experienced group that was very close-knit.

"The offensive line was made up of people from different backgrounds as far as family," Phil stated. "All of us depended on each other. The guy I played next to, Chuck Edge, we knew what each other was going to do on any play…We had responsibilities. We had to know who played in front of us and who the backup was. We ran the Houston veer, which we had different responsibilities. It wasn't always block the man in front of you.

"We didn't get lots of recognition," Phil continued, "but what we did was we started the play. Without what we had done, those things wouldn't have happened."

The largest player on the starting offensive line, as far as listed weight, was Jess Croley at 200 pounds. The smallest was Chuck Edge, who was listed at 170 but by the state championship against Bellville, he had slipped to 148. The center, Bob Skipwith, weighed 165. Phil Lemons, who was dubbed "Bear" by Coach Ken Ard, weighed in at 185 pounds and may have been outweighed by some of his opponents, but at 6-3, very few of the defensive players he lined up against had him beaten in the height department.

"Throughout district and pre-district, we were clearly outweighed and outmanned through the line," Bob Skipwith said. "We were relatively small. We liked to pride ourselves on being quick on the first couple of steps out of the box. None of us were fast, but we were quick off the ball. I think that helped us to overcome a lot of the size issues."

Ronnie Cross said of the line that played in front of him, "You know, as a quarterback, nothing starts without those guys. I never was very good anyway, but I really wouldn't have been good on my back sideways. Realistically, when you think about it, if the quarterback doesn't get the snap, what else can happen? It all starts right in the center of the line, and those cats on either side of him. They don't get the press or the notoriety that they need or they should get, but without those guys, nothing would have ever happened.

"The thing about our line that always impressed me is there wasn't anything special about them. They weren't big, they weren't fast, they weren't overpoweringly quick, or just outstandingly strong like the guys you see nowadays. But when they blew off the football, the line of scrimmage was three yards down the field. That's where it started. If it was on the 40 and we snapped the football, and we're going toward the goal line, the line of scrimmage was at the 37. They did that good of a job. I got sacked, and there was always all that stuff, but for the most part, if I got sacked, I didn't have to get up and yell at anybody. I never did that. If I got sacked for the most part, they were back there picking me up, the guy that let him through, and telling me, 'Sorry about that.' And it was more of a 'get him next time' because that's just football."

In the backfield behind the quarterback, the Pirates had a number of solid choices with which to run the ball. Seniors Wendell Collins and Wayne Tyson had been a one-two punch out of the Pirates' backfield on the 1976 team. They had proven they were not afraid to get down into the trenches and fight. Wayne, who carried the nickname "Tottie," had scored the first three Wylie touchdowns over a period of three games in the new Pirate Stadium in 1976. Despite Wendell's diminutive nickname, "The Mighty Mite," as one of the local papers called him, he knew where to find the holes and had a knack for making the big play.

There were plenty of people to carry the ball, but as the season started, the coaches were still undecided as to who would get to run with it the most. Besides the tandem of Wendell and Wayne, the Pirates had Wayne Mayberry, Dale Morgan and Dan Whitt—as well as the option of the quarterback—to run the ball with using the veer offense. Wayne Mayberry was the biggest of all of the Pirate running backs, weighing in at 160 pounds. The coaching staff eventually settled on Wayne Mayberry and Wendell Collins as the starters in the backfield.

Then there were the receivers. Guys like Roy Fuentes, Roy McClendon and Tony Garner at the flanker position and Doug Gollahon, Garth Touchstone, Mark Whitehead and Rickey Blackman at tight end provided formidable and able targets for which to aim. The Houston veer offense which the Pirates ran used the tight ends as the primary targets (the offense used a tight end on each side of the box lining up) though the Pirates had plenty of sure-handed flankers. In fact, any of the aforementioned receivers had the hands to make game-breaking catches. Some ended up doing just that in 1977.

The passing game turned out to be a huge part of Wylie's offense in 1977, something that was seldom found in high school football teams in Texas in those days.

Tony Garner recalled, "Most teams, outside of us, were not throwing teams—not in 2A football back then. We were running the Houston veer, and Ronnie and Rock could throw the ball, and there were five or six of us that pretty much could catch about anything. And Shaffer wasn't afraid to chunk the ball, either."

Receivers coach Bruce King said of the Pirates' passing offense, "It was just a matter of necessity, I think. It was what gave us a chance to win. When we were a little bit outmanned at times, we felt like that was one of the big things that gave us a little bit of an edge—our ability to keep possession of the ball on offense and move the ball offensively. We couldn't line up a lot of times and feel like we could just run straight at people and be successful."

On defense, the Pirates were every bit as gritty as the offense. The Wylie defenders hit hard and played smart. Seniors Jess Croley and Danny Schultz, the two defensive ends, stood out as leaders of the Pirate defense, epitomizing what the Pirates played for.

Perhaps it is fitting that Danny and Jess played on opposite ends of the defensive line, for their styles were as different as night and day. Jess typically let his play on the field do the talking for him and led by example, while Danny was more vocal. There they were, in every game—Danny on the right end of the defensive line, Jess on the left. Like bookends.

"Jess Croley was the defensive end I played behind all the time," said Rickey Blackman, a junior who played most of the season at one of the outside linebacker positions. "He was a senior, and an awesome player, and I really enjoyed playing behind him."

"Jess was more of a silent kind of guy," Roy Fuentes explained. "Our emotional, get-crazy-kind-of-guy was Danny Schultz. He was the guy that when we needed to be fired up, he was there to push us, to kick us, to yell at us, to do whatever. He was the guy that was the vocal leader of the team on the defensive side...he was a very gritty guy. He played all out, 110 percent on every play. When we needed to play physical, or when we needed an intimidator in the middle, Danny was the guy who was going to be the intimidator."

"(Danny) was pretty wild," Jess said. "He wasn't that big. Actually, none of us were that big. But Danny was pretty wired. He was kind of hard-headed. He had a big head, too. He deserves to be in the Hall of Fame, because anybody that can get a head like that in a football helmet, they deserve to be there."

Starting at the defensive tackle positions between Jess and Danny were two tough juniors, Chuck Edge on the left side and Tim Pelton on the right. Behind the defensive line, at linebacker, the Pirates began the season with Garth Touchstone in the middle and Rock King and Mark Whitehead at the outside positions. After the second game of the season when Rock re-injured his shoulder and could no longer play defense, Rickey Blackman stepped into an outside linebacker position and performed admirably.

The secondary, when completely healthy, was as good as any 2A secondary in the area. The defensive backs might not have been the speediest, but they knew the other team's tendencies, took the best routes to get to the ball and often they got there before the receiver did. The Pirates used Dale Morgan at left cornerback and Roy Fuentes at right corner, with Wayne Mayberry at free safety and Tony Garner at strong safety. All four starting secondary members also rotated in on offense for the Pirates—Tony and Roy at flanker and Wayne and Dale at running back.

Tony was a returning letterman who had an amazing 19 interceptions for the Pirates in 1976, a total that ranks him fifth all time on the single season list for Texas high school football. He played only sporadically in the first three games of the 1977 season due to a pulled groin muscle, but once he got going in the fourth game of the season (against Justin Northwest), he proved to be unstoppable. Roy McClendon and Rickey Blackman filled the gap at strong safety while Tony was injured.

Though they were not going to blow anybody away with size or speed, the Pirates were talented in many of the intangible areas that often escaped the opponents' scouting reports. Among those intangibles were outstanding technique and excellent recognition, or the ability to read a play.

"Talent-wise, there wasn't any real reason to be where we ended up," Coach Page said. "What we had were a bunch of kids that wanted to win, that got along great together. There was a great chemistry on that team. Everybody had bought into our system. The thing that we could do is we could play technique. The kids did things the way we asked them to. When we were coaching them on film, and when you stepped with the wrong foot here, they worked their tails off in practice to make sure they stepped with the right foot. And they just did things right, and in the end, that made the difference. We were able to beat teams with really superior physical talent because we did things right and didn't make mistakes."

Another of the intangibles that the Pirates had going for them was mental preparation.

"They were really dedicated to learning," secondary/receivers coach Bruce King said. "They did a lot of study on film, and we did, not only as a staff, but as a team. Even individually, a lot of those kids, during their study halls, back at that time, those films were available. So they looked at an awful lot of film and studied individually a lot."

The Wylie defense employed a technique different from most football teams of the day at any level. Rather than have all the defensive linemen commit themselves to immediately rushing the quarterback, they did essentially the same thing as the offense—once the ball was snapped, they read the play. And as soon as they recognized where the ball was going, after reading the "keys" or clues from the offensive linemen, they went for the ball and bypassed the often much larger blockers. The idea was to "control the gap, then flow to the ball," according to Chuck Edge.

This technique would effectively neutralize any size advantage the opponent's offensive line might have over Wylie's defensive line. "You would have your bags packed and ready to go," Coach Shaffer described. "This big brut across from you did not mean jack to you if you didn't have to take him on. If you can recognize quickly enough (where the ball is), you can just go to the ball. That is essentially what run defense always has been and still is, for that matter."

"We relied on a lot of quickness and movement and stunts and things like that," Jess Croley explained. "I think we were a lot better than people gave us credit for, but we weren't a show-stopper or anything."

With only about 31 players on the roster (not counting junior varsity players who were brought up for the playoffs), many Pirates played both ways. Chuck Edge, Jess Croley, Wayne Mayberry, Roy Fuentes, Roy McClendon, Garth Touchstone, Mark Whitehead, Tony Garner, Rickey Blackman and Dale Morgan were just a few of the Pirates who saw action on both offense and defense.

As with any championship team, the part the role players played on the 1977 Pirates could not be underestimated. Players like Troy Ripple, Jimmy Hughes, Paul Adams, Kevin Adams, Jack Hirmon and many others stepped in when called on to fill roles when needed. Coach Page recalled that when the team lined up for tackling drills in practice, players would count where they lined up so they would not have to line up against Jimmy Hughes, one of the strongest and hardest hitters on the Pirates. Late in the season, sophomore Mike Helm, another role player, became a factor at defensive tackle when Tim Pelton went down in the playoffs with a broken leg. Junior Bruce Cryer did the same for the Pirates at middle linebacker when Garth Touchstone injured his knee against Granbury in the first playoff game.

The role players were part of the scout team, which ran live scrimmages against the starters in practice during the week. The scout team would line up against the starters and run plays from the upcoming opponent's playbook, and in these live scrimmages, the scout team would often push the starters, one of the unsung things that contributed immensely to the success of the 1977 Wylie Pirates.

"You're trying to kick their (the starters') butts, 'cause it's for their own good," said Jack Hirmon, a backup flanker/cornerback and special teams coverage man who was a member of the scout team. "If you're not playing hard and not making them work, then you're not doing your job. Your job is to make them better."

Despite the team's size and speed disadvantages, no one questioned the Pirates' desire or toughness. For the 1977 Pirates, guys often played sick. Guys played injured. Guys did what it took to win.

These Pirates, particularly the seniors, had been through thick and thin together over the years growing up in the small Texas town. Many of them had played football in Wylie with or against each other as early as the fourth grade in the pee wee football division of the Wylie Sports Association. Tony Garner remembered that many of the seniors from the 1977 team often gathered in his front yard to play football when they were in the fourth and fifth grade, since most of them lived within a couple of blocks of each other in Wylie at that time and throughout their adolescent years. They spent a great deal of time together while growing up.

"Being in a small town, we hung out during the week at night, and especially on weekends," Phil Lemons said. "Lake Lavon is real close. In the summertime and up until the winter when it gets so cold that you couldn't, we would usually gather at the lake. We were real close."

In addition to being familiar with each other and one another's tendencies, these seniors were familiar with how Coach Shaffer's system and coaching style worked; they had been operating it for three years. In fact, according to center Bob Skipwith, in the summer of 1974, the incoming freshmen were allowed to work out with the high school team in order to become familiar with the new head coach's system.

Defensive tackle/offensive guard Chuck Edge recalled, "We were all so different. There was one of everybody from every kind of walk of life, really. But we were real tight. Real tight."

So tight, in fact, that many members of the team worked out much of the summer together, practicing plays, going over fundamentals and running routes—in the extreme Texas heat, on their own, without the direction of the Wylie High School coaching staff. When it came time for two-a-days in early August, most, if not all, of the Pirates were in shape, Ronnie Cross remembered.

"We did a lot of work in the off-season and in the summers," Ronnie said. "We had a lot of people up there working and running and catching passes from me. I'd throw the football 250, 300 times a day every day of the week, and run the option. I'd have 25 guys up there running routes for me. Linemen, linebackers—it didn't matter who they were. We did that on our own without any coaches or anything during the summers. When we came into two-a-days, it was on our minds. It was on our minds to win the district championship and to win the state championship."

Doug Gollahon moved to Wylie in the summer of 1977 ahead of his parents. His family stayed behind in Burleson for a few extra days to wrap up some loose ends. During that brief period, Doug stayed with Rock and his family. The first night Doug stayed with the Kings, Rock told him they were going up to the high school. At first, Doug did not know why, but it did not take him long to catch on.

"Every night up at the high school, nearly everybody was up there working out," Doug explained. "We would lift weights for a little while, then we'd go out on the field and have a big touch football game. I just don't remember any of the guys not being there. Everybody showed up. That's the kind of stuff that it takes to be successful."

The players on this team, for the most part, had spent the previous three years becoming familiar with Coach Shaffer's system and in particular the veer offense. And the seniors on the 1977 team understood the intricacies of how it worked, a strength that came out early in the playoffs when Ronnie Cross emerged as the No. 1 quarterback. Ronnie became a master of running Coach Shaffer's veer offense, as was evidenced by his play on the field—especially in the state championship game against Bellville.

One of the things that made the Pirates difficult to stop in 1977 is that the team did not have just one go-to player. This proved advantageous because often opponents did not know who to key in on.

"We really didn't have any one person (for the opponent to concentrate on)," Phil Lemons recalled. "When someone scouted us, I don't think they would say, 'You have to stop this guy to win the game.'"

The Coaches

No one could deny that Wylie was an extremely well-coached team.

With Coach Shaffer calling the offensive plays, Coach Rick Page (who had been a four-year letterman at offensive center for Austin College in Sherman, Texas) calling the shots on defense and coaching the offensive line, Coach Bruce King handling the defensive secondary and the receivers, and Coach Ken Ard (a carryover from Coach Gerald Lloyd's staff) coaching the defensive ends and offensive tackles, this coaching staff was easily one of the best in the business.

Nearly everyone on that Wylie coaching staff knew at least one other member of the staff before coming to Wylie. Coach Page had previously worked with Coach Shaffer when they were both on the same staff at Sherman High School, in the same town where they both went to college. Coach Page had played football at Austin College alongside Bruce King and Hardee McCrary, who coached in Wylie in 1974-75, in the early 1970s. In the summer of 1977, Coach Page recruited a former college football teammate, Dick Matkin, to handle some of the junior varsity coaching and varsity scouting duties at Wylie High School (Coach Matkin was also the Pirates' head basketball coach).

All of these coaches were tireless workers. From late Friday night on through Saturday and up to Monday morning, these guys were studying game film and trying to figure out what the team needed to do to get better.

"They were an amazing coaching staff," Doug Gollahon recalled. "They worked really well together. They were definitely ahead of their time. They had unbelievable work habits."

Coach Page recalled that at age 28 in 1977, he was different from all the other coaches in that he was single; hence, football was his whole life. He often worked into the wee hours of the morning during football season. Everyone in town knew his car, so when they saw it parked at the field house late, they did not think anything of it. When he got a new car and the police spotted it parked outside the field house late one night, they became suspicious and went in to see who was at the field house.

Indeed, Coach Page spent most of his time that season at the field house studying films to prepare for Wylie's next game.

"It was before computers," Phil Lemons said. "He used to take every play and put it on a card, then he'd punch the card in a way that he'd sort through 'em. He would know the tendencies before Monday when we'd get our scouting report."

"They worked a lot of hours we never saw," Ronnie Cross recalled. "Come Monday morning when we got through with the game, we had a scouting report on that next team, from the junior high coaches going out and watching 'em. We all knew who we were up against, what they did best, what they didn't do best. Our coaches always had us prepared to play anything or anybody."

This coaching staff noticed every little thing, even right down to opponents' linemen's stances, according to Chuck Edge. Not much got by them when it came to the opposition. And they certainly knew how to motivate their players.

Roy Fuentes said that members of the team would often meet at the home of Bruce King and watch films of the upcoming opponent. These coaches would spot everything in the other team—their strengths, their weaknesses, their tendencies. They could also see what they needed to correct in their own team.

Coach Shaffer was trained in physics, hence he was smarter than the average coach. He had been the valedictorian of his high school class in Leonard, Texas, some 15 years before he became the head football coach in Wylie. In 1990, two years after he left Wylie, Coach Shaffer earned a PhD in physics from East Texas State University (later Texas A&M Commerce).

Percentages and details often played into the way Coach Shaffer called his offensive schemes. His offensive genius combined with the defensive genius of Coach Page—and the players executing the plays—made the 1977 Wylie Pirates virtually unstoppable.

"(Shaffer) was really smart," Chuck Edge remembered. "He was more into psychology than the physical stuff. Everybody wants to have a great big player that runs fast and all that stuff. But he really touched on the psychological part of the game…and as great a genius as Shaffer was on offense, Page was every bit that good on defense."

Of his longtime coaching colleague, Rick Page said, "Jerry is one of the most unique and best human beings that I've ever been around in my life. Jerry took that young staff, and he gave each one of us things to do, and showed us how to go about doing things the way they ought to be done…he found a bunch of people that were willing to work and molded us into a staff that was really unbelievable when you think about it. The same kind of camaraderie that the kids had for each other, we had as a staff. There wasn't any bickering; we just rolled up our sleeves and went to work. I attribute a great deal of that to Jerry Shaffer."

Each assistant had his own contribution to make this coaching staff a successful one. They were all master teachers. They knew when to get onto the kids, but perhaps most important, they knew when to praise them. They made the team line up and run wind sprints only once that season to discipline the team for a bad practice, according to Ronnie Cross.

Each coach seemed to have his own area or areas where his strengths lay. According to Roy Fuentes, each member of the coaching staff had an area of "specialization."

"We were taught really well," Jack Hirmon said of Wylie's coaching staff. "They were great teachers. And we did it over and over and over and over again until we got it right."

Ronnie Cross recalled, "I think the coaches had the ability to make us feel like we were really, truly better than what we really were. Shaffer had a way about pushing a hot button or motivating us to the fact that we could overcome anything, we could climb the mountain, we could stand on top, and we could see...we could see we were the best.

"That's really the key," Ronnie went on. "We had great coaching. I mean, Shaffer was ahead of his time. This guy, I can remember him sitting out there in practice and we'd see a big old cloud pop up like this in the west, and we'd think, 'Alright, we're going to get rained out here in about two minutes.' He'd be sitting there looking at his watch and timing the cloud, and he's saying 45 minutes. And he never missed it. He was within three minutes either way. We're sitting there saying, 'There ain't no way. Ten minutes, and we're out of here.' But he was right on."

It was apparent that Wylie's strength lay not just in the intelligence of its players, but its coaches as well.

"Basically, everyone we went on the field against was clearly outcoached," Bob Skipwith recalled. "It boiled down to drill after drill after drill, making the right move, thinking what your steps were and where you needed to be and understanding that...playing as a team versus a bunch of guys out there doing their own thing."

Coach Shaffer ran a tight ship. His rules were his rules, and he never budged from them, as evidenced by the David Leopard incident. The kids respected Coach Shaffer and the staff because, in spite of their youthfulness, they were men who had earned that respect.

"Coach Shaffer was very disciplined, very well respected," Bob Skipwith said. "You never saw anybody talking back to any of them, to my knowledge. I think we knew there was a price to pay if you did anything that went against the rules, and he enforced the rules, and he didn't care what anybody else had to say."

There were no big egos on the 1977 Wylie Pirates, simply because the coaches would not allow it. The team always came first, and players who were not willing to put the team first were not fit to be Wylie Pirates.

As the cliché goes, a football team is a chain, and a chain is only as strong as its weakest link. On this Wylie team, there were simply no weak links. Every man played his part and played it well, because every player put the team first—even at the sacrifice of his own playing time or any other kind of personal gain.

"It was all a team effort. There wasn't any 'star,'" Ronnie said. "Just because I played quarterback, I wasn't anything. Rock King was as good as or better than I was. The way I look at it, (quarterback) was just a position, just like the other 10. It took all 11 of us to get it done, and we understood that, and I think the coaches understood that."

According to Tony Garner, "I don't think anybody believed that they were the all-star of the team. I believe everybody thought that everybody played an equal part in the game. Everybody had their position and their skills set up, and they had their slot on that team to fill. And everybody had a position to fill, and did. For the most part, I don't remember anybody dogging somebody about blowing a play. Shaffer didn't put up with that."

Some of the lessons Coach Shaffer taught his football players could be applied to life and not just football. To this day, Phil Lemons said, Shaffer's scripted practice schedule has helped him a great deal in his business ventures.

"He'd outline practices, and they had it scripted," Phil described. "Every five minutes, they would change, or continue what they were doing. That's one thing that made him different, because he cared about little things."

"That group of coaches was a unique and a special group of guys," Rock King recalled. "Certainly, they prepared that team week in and week out, not just physically, but psychologically and emotionally. They got them ready to play at a level that they got a whole lot more out of them than most coaching staffs would have been able to. I think it was because of the unique combination of coaches. Coach Page and my brother, Bruce King, were probably the emotional, spiritual drives, a lot more intense than some of the other coaches. Coach Shaffer seemed to be more cerebral, and Xs and Os, although he had his moments."

These Pirate players clearly took on the personality of their coaches. The Pirates always thought on their feet, hence they played smart football. And like the coaches, the Pirate players were tireless workers.

"We worked hard," Jess Croley stated. "There were times when we'd be out there practicing from 2:30 to 9:30 at night. We'd stay out there quite a while sometimes. They would be turning on the lights at Pirate Stadium.

"I believe we were the best prepared," Jess continued. "We had the most 'want to,' I guess. We had a bunch of boys that wanted to (win). I tend to think of it as we all had hearts like nine-pound hammers. That was a big part of it right there."

Game One, Wylie vs. Diamond Hill

The Pirates' two opponents in scrimmage games were Princeton, a small Collin County town just west of Farmersville, and Seagoville, a suburb near South Dallas. Both games gave the Pirates reason to be optimistic. Seagoville, which competed in the 3A classification, was a much bigger school than Wylie enrollment-wise and the Pirates had held their own against them.

In one scrimmage game, Doug Gollahon ran the wrong route on a pass play but still caught the ball and scored a touchdown, a possible signal that 1977 was going to be the Wylie Pirates' year.

"When I got back to the sideline, (Coach Shaffer) informed me that if I'm ever going to run the wrong route again, to make sure I score," Doug recalled.

Both Ronnie and Rock played well at quarterback in practice and in the two scrimmage games. When it came right down to who was going to be the starting quarterback, "we could not make up our minds," Coach Shaffer remembered. "What we decided we'd do is alternate them in predistrict. We decided by the first district game (fifth game of the season), we'd have a starter."

In the meantime, for the season opener, Coach Shaffer had to decide who would start under center. He had discussed the matter with both Ronnie and Rock at length. At the end of the day, his senior, Ronnie Cross, got the call to take the field as the Pirates' starting quarterback against Fort Worth Diamond Hill. The Pirates were originally scheduled to play at Rockwall in the opener—the UIL realigns district every two years, and 1977 was a non-realignment year. Football teams kept the same schedules for both years after realignment with the sites flip-flopped from one year to the next, hence the Pirates were set to play the same schedule in 1977 as they played in 1976, only with the sites reversed. Following that format, the Pirates' first three games of 1977 would have been all on the road at Rockwall, Kaufman and Farmersville. But Rockwall moved up a classification to 3A in midstream and changed schedules, something that seldom happens in the UIL, leaving Wylie to find a replacement game for their season opener.

Fort Worth Diamond Hill, like the Seagoville team Wylie had scrimmaged, was a 3A school much larger than Wylie as far as enrollment went. But Diamond Hill was not one of the stronger 3A teams. In fact, just a few years after playing Wylie in the 1977 opener, they lost 41 consecutive games from 1982–85 to tie Beeville for the sixth longest losing streak in Texas high school football history.

As the season started, Wylie was missing a key defensive player in strong safety Tony Garner, who was out with a pulled groin muscle. As thin as the Pirates' roster was, any injury to a starter was going to be a blow to the team.

"We didn't have an awful lot of depth at very many positions, so anybody that was injured or not able to play for any reason would have been a concern from week to week," secondary coach Bruce King recalled.

The town of Wylie collectively held its breath as the Pirates kicked off the 1977 season at home. Would the Pirates, now ranked in the top 10 in the state by the Associated Press, be able to repeat the success of the 1976 team and take it further? How would Ronnie Cross fare in his debut as the starting quarterback? Did the Pirates have enough depth in the defensive backfield to offset the loss of injured strong safety Tony Garner? Would this defense be able to force turnovers and limit the scoring opportunities of larger, quicker opponents?

Was the 1976 season a fluke?

Before 8 p.m. on September 2, 1977, only questions existed. By 11 p.m., most, if not all, of those questions had been answered.

Ronnie threw four touchdown passes in the first half, and the Pirates gained more than 350 total yards of offense on their way to a 53-14 shellacking of the Diamond Hill Eagles (ironically, it was the same score by which Bowie had eliminated the Pirates in the regional playoffs the year before). The maroon and white defensive attack forced eight turnovers (five interceptions, three fumbles) from Diamond Hill. Leading the way on defense were Rock King (playing at outside linebacker) with two interceptions and Danny Schultz with two fumble recoveries.

The Wylie passing game clicked on all cylinders in the first 24 minutes of play. Ronnie connected with Doug Gollahon with 2:45 left in the first quarter for the first score of the game, and junior Rickey Blackman—who began the season as the Pirates' place-kicker—tacked on the extra point. Early in the second period, Ronnie hit Roy Fuentes for the second TD, this one covering 25 yards, and Rickey added the PAT to make it 14-0 in favor of Wylie. Ronnie hooked up with junior tight end Garth Touchstone for two more touchdowns in the second quarter, from eight and six yards out, and the rout was on. Though the Eagles blocked the PAT after both of Garth's scoring plays, the Pirates took a comfortable 26-0 lead to the locker room.

Ronnie Cross recalled that the Pirates gained huge amounts of yardage using a seam route to the tight end after checking off of Diamond Hill's free safety, who was playing up close to the line of scrimmage. "It was just there. He'd bite on the run, and before he knew what was going on, our tight end was past him and wide open…we just ate him up with that play all night long, if I remember right."

It was more of the same in the second half, though Diamond Hill caught a break when Wayne Tyson fumbled the second half kickoff and gave the Eagles the short field to work with. Diamond Hill quarterback Tony Hazle scored the team's first touchdown of the game on an option play, and the Pirates blocked the extra point attempt.

The Pirates answered that drive with their first rushing touchdown of the game, this one from Wendell Collins (the PAT attempt was no good), and the maroon and white held a 32-6 lead.

With the game in hand, Coach Shaffer began to substitute freely, and Rock King took over for Ronnie under center. Rock wasted no time in finding Doug Gollahon for a 12-yard touchdown, and Rickey's kick made it 39-6, Pirates.

At this point, not much was going wrong for the Pirates. This team even had a way of turning apparent disasters into good fortune. Late in the third quarter when Rickey Blackman was about to cross the goal line with yet another Pirate touchdown, the Eagles stripped the ball from him. Danny Schultz pounced on the ball in the end zone for the score, and Rickey's PAT kick put the Pirates on top by a 46-6 count.

Diamond Hill did not quit, however. Mike Flores scored from four yards out in the fourth quarter, and Hazle found John Diaz for the two-point conversion to pull the Eagles to within 46-14. But Rock King and Co. had the answer.

Rock found tight end Mark Whitehead on a pass-run play covering 33 yards late in the game for the Pirates' last touchdown of the evening. Rickey's extra point provided the final margin of 53-14.

The win moved Wylie up to No. 7 in the Associated Press state poll. Though they had won decisively over Diamond Hill, Coach Shaffer admitted that he was not ready to proclaim the 1977 Pirates had arrived just yet, since Diamond Hill was not one of the stronger teams in the 3A classification.

"Whatever we did, in terms of statistics, was meaningless," the coach explained. "We got somewhat of an idea, but we didn't gain a whole lot from the Diamond Hill game. It didn't help us a lot."

"Our coaches, I think, always did a good job of keeping us on an even keel on a big win or after a loss," Rock King remembered. "Part of the thing they always stressed is learning from your experiences in the game and improving on the things that you need to improve on, and executing. Even though you might outscore an opponent by a wide margin, there's a lot of things you could work on, and certainly during film sessions, they broke that down and made it pretty evident."

With a 1-0 record, the Pirates were ready for their next non-district contest. This one was going to be against their old nemesis, the Kaufman Lions. Kaufman was one of the top 2A teams in the state that year and was always a tough test for the Wylie Pirates.

Game Two, Wylie vs. Kaufman

The Pirates had historically had problems with the Kaufman Lions. Just a year earlier, Kaufman had topped Wylie, 14-8, in the second game ever at the new Pirate Stadium. The Lions won handily when the two teams met in 1974 and 1975.

What occurred on the night of September 9, 1977, in Kaufman between the Pirates and the Lions was very different from the previous year's meeting between the two, which was a low-scoring affair dominated by defense. This was a new year, and the Wylie-Kaufman showdown (played at Nossman Field in Kaufman) resulted in the classic slugfest. Kaufman eventually won the offensive shootout, 53-33, though the Pirates proved their resilience by not giving up after losing two front-line players to injury on this extremely hot, humid Texas Friday night.

The Pirates actually held a 13-0 lead over the Lions early in the game before Kaufman's diminutive (5-5, 150 pounds) but speedy running back Roger Jones (a.k.a. "Peely") took center stage, jump-starting that team's offense. Behind Jones, the Lions scored 21 consecutive points to gain a 21-13 advantage over the Pirates heading into the intermission.

The Pirates still hung in there. They cut the deficit to two early in the third quarter when defensive end Jess Croley grabbed a Lions fumble out of the air and ran it 20 yards to paydirt. The two-point conversion attempt was no good.

"That was a fluke, actually," Jess said of his fumble recovery for a touchdown. "It bounced off their running back, Peely Jones. It was a pitchout, and it bounced off his shoulder, and bounced up and hit me right in the hands."

It proved to be one of Jess's proudest moments of his high school football career. He started for two years on both the offensive and defensive lines for Wylie, and his touchdown against Kaufman was the only one he scored.

The Lions scored twice in the third period and took a 33-19 lead into the fourth quarter. But the Pirates stayed close, this time with a touchdown pass from Ronnie Cross to Doug Gollahon. Rickey Blackman added the extra point that pulled the Pirates to within seven at 33-26 with 10:31 left to play in the game.

Unfortunately for the Pirates, it was as close as they got. Behind the running of Peely Jones, Kaufman rattled off 20 points in the fourth quarter to put the game out of reach.

The Wylie offense remained impressive; 33 points would be enough to win on most nights (Wendell Collins, Doug Gollahon and Garth Touchstone also scored touchdowns for Wylie). The Kaufman offense, however, was too much for the Pirate defense on that particular night. The Lions had Lady Luck on their side, too; twice they scored on plays on which a receiver grabbed a pass that had been tipped by one or more Wylie defenders.

"In the first quarter, we were already ahead," Wayne Mayberry recalled. "Then that game kind of got a little out of hand. We had a lot of mistakes trying to intercept balls, and tipping 'em right into their hands. That was an interesting game. It was an eye opener."

But in the end, it was the speed of Peely Jones—along with a powerful blocking back named Ronald Trammell leading the way—that proved to be too much for the Pirate defense to overcome. "It was hard to get your hands on (Jones), and he was a strong runner, too, for his size," Rock King explained, "so even after you got your hands on him, he was hard to bring down. We certainly didn't have anybody that could simulate the kind of explosion and speed that he had. They had not just him, but several players that were dominating."

"He was so good," Coach Shaffer said of Peely Jones. "We couldn't tackle him, and no one else could that year. There's no telling how many yards he had. He probably averaged 12 or 15 yards a carry that year. He was incredible."

Wayne Mayberry, who played free safety for the Pirates, was one of those faced with the task of trying to stop Peely Jones. "We'd try and go to tackle him, then he'd make a move," Wayne recalled. "If you weren't in the position to go back whichever way he was going, you'd go right off the side of him."

Peely rushed for a total of 196 yards on just 18 attempts in that game against Wylie, which meant he gained an average of almost 11 yards each time he ran the football. As a team, Kaufman racked up more than 550 yards of offense.

Probably as a result of the Kaufman game, Wayne Mayberry, who was most likely the Pirates' fastest running back, was tagged "Peely" later in the season by his Pirate teammates.

By the middle of the third quarter, Wylie had several second and third string players in the game and even some starters playing out of position. The heat and humidity forced many substitutions that otherwise would not have been made, something that turned out to be a blessing in disguise for the Pirates—they were able to use that game to determine what needs the team needed to address the most on the field.

One of the things the coaches found out as a result of that game was that Doug Gollahon could help the team more as a tight end than he could as a linebacker. Doug had entered the game as the weak side linebacker in place of Rock King, who left the game after receiving a blow that irritated his surgically repaired left shoulder. The play on which Rock was injured turned out to be the last down he played on defense that season.

One of the changes the coaches made after this Kaufman game was moving Rickey Blackman from strong safety to linebacker, a move that paid dividends for the Pirates.

"Coach Shaffer figured out I needed a different position (after the Kaufman game)," Rickey said with a laugh. "He obviously was right, because we ended up getting the right mix in the secondary, and linebacker ended up being a good position for me."

The Pirates and their fans endured a frightening moment late in the game when they saw their quarterback, Ronnie Cross, hit the Kaufman turf awkwardly with about a minute left to play. Weighing all of 145 pounds, Ronnie was hit in the backfield by a 220-pound defensive end who had grabbed him by the facemask and slung him to the ground.

"From what I remember, I landed on my face," Ronnie recalled. "My back bowed up pretty good back behind me. The next thing I remember is our coaching staff and Kaufman's coaching staff and everybody on the field. The next thing I remember, my parents were on the field. The next thing I remember, we were in the ambulance going away. We had a blowout in the ambulance on the way to the hospital, and that was about how my night went."

Rock King was unavailable to play quarterback, having re-injured his shoulder earlier in the contest. This forced the third-string signal caller, junior Bruce "Doc" Cryer, into action. Still, the Pirates did not quit despite being down by more than 20 points in the game's waning moments.

"To have them come back on you and score 53 points…I think most teams would have gave up. But we just kept on 'em," Wayne Mayberry remembered.

The Pirates were able to move the ball with Bruce under center, and Wayne Mayberry scored the Pirates' final touchdown of the game from a yard out with less than a minute to go.

Still, the Pirates and their fans received another scare when Bruce Cryer was injured after being tackled. Some Kaufman defenders combined to pinch something near his pelvic area, and after icing his injury on the sidelines for a few minutes, Bruce became the second Wylie Pirate that night to make a trip to the hospital in an ambulance.

"I got sandwiched between two defensive tacklers," Bruce recalled. "I just laid out there and I finally decided to have it checked out. It turned out to be nothing, hardly. It was just sore for a few days. I strained some ligaments, I think."

In the game account in one of the local newspapers, Coach Shaffer praised the efforts of his team, and particularly for scoring 33 points against a very good Kaufman squad that went on to finish the regular season at 10-0 that year. Looking back on that game many years later, he had the same recollection.

"We had kids with cramps, and throwing up on the sidelines from getting too hot and sweating so much," Coach Shaffer remembered. "We were pumping water into 'em the best we could. It was a miserable night for our kids. But we got to see a lot of different kids in a lot of different situations, and that really helped us...it was a tremendous experience for us to build on."

In the first two weeks of the season, the Pirates played one of the weaker 3A teams and blew them out, then played one of the best 2A teams in the state on a very hot, humid night and scored 33 points but allowed 53. Because of the circumstances under which they played the Kaufman game, as well as Diamond Hill the week prior, Coach Shaffer said neither game was an accurate measuring stick for how the Pirates' season would turn out.

"The conclusions you drew about how good we were against Diamond Hill would have been way off," the head coach explained. "You're not getting a true picture at all. Against Kaufman, you wouldn't have gotten a true picture, either. That was just as misleading."

The loss to Kaufman knocked Wylie out of the Associated Press state top 10 poll. But this was not the time to be concerned with polls—what the Pirates needed was to start winning ballgames. With a 1-1 record, now the Pirates were set to head just a few miles northeast up Highway 78 to take on their old rivals, the Farmersville Farmers.

Game Three, Wylie vs. Farmersville

It was just a few years removed from being one of the most intense Texas high school football rivalries of the time. Wylie and Farmersville were district opponents years earlier when Wylie was a Class A school. By 1977, Wylie was beginning to outgrow Farmersville in terms of enrollment (after 1977, they did not play each other again until 1986). From 1972 to 1977, though the Pirates and Farmers did not play in the same district, they were still rivals. Only about 15 miles of highway separated the two high schools.

Besides having a powerful football team, Farmersville has another claim to fame. It was the home of World War II hero Audie Murphy.

By 1977, the Wylie-Farmersville rivalry had cooled somewhat, since many of the kids on the two schools' athletic teams knew each other and had become friends over the years.

"We had played baseball against those (Wylie) kids since the time we were in grade school," said Bobby Bishop, the Farmers' quarterback in 1977. "We knew 'em really well. It was really good to see 'em do as well as they did. In the olden days, Wylie-Farmersville was a pretty hated rivalry, but really with this group, we knew 'em well and got along with 'em."

Farmersville had yet to move up to the 2A classification; in 1977, the Farmers were a Class A powerhouse. In fact, they began the season as favorites to win District 15-A. In week two, just before they took on Wylie, the Farmers clobbered Van Alstyne, 39-0. Like Kaufman, Farmersville went on to finish the regular season at 10-0 in 1977.

A 7-0 win over Farmersville had given the Pirates their first victory at the new stadium in the third game of the 1976 season. Typically, Wylie and Farmersville played close, down-to-the-wire, smash-mouth games.

Game three in 1977 was no exception. On September 16, the Pirates traveled to a muddy Farmer Stadium and lost a squeaker, 14-12. In that game, the Pirate defense contained the Farmers' star running back, Tony Craddock, who was used to tearing up defenses with 100-plus yard games. Tony gained just 65 yards on

19 carries against Wylie, and 33 of those yards came on one play (Tony's cousin, Mike Craddock, starred at middle linebacker for the Pirates on the 1976 bi-district champion team).

With the Pirate defense zoning in on Tony Craddock, players like Kevin Shinn and Bobby Bishop picked up the slack for Farmersville on offense while Elvin Taylor and Kevin Saffell carried the purple and gold defense. Bobby, the Farmers' quarterback, completed four of five passes for 68 yards in the first half. He also ran the ball 11 times for 41 yards in the first 24 minutes.

Fortunately for the Pirates, neither Ronnie's nor Rock's injury from the week before was serious enough to sideline him, and Ronnie Cross started under center against the Farmers.

Wylie had the ball first and gained a first down, but a promising drive ended when Elvin Taylor sacked Ronnie for a nine-yard loss on third down. Rock King's short 13-yard punt to the Farmersville 41 gave the Farmers excellent field position for their first drive.

The Farmers scored on the ensuing drive with a six-yard touchdown run by Kevin Shinn, set up by a 42-yard completion from Bobby Bishop to Matt Lee. Dale Morgan crashed through and blocked the extra point attempt, leaving the Farmers with a 6-0 lead.

Late in the first quarter, the Farmers' Mark Wilcoxson recovered a Wylie fumble on the Pirate 16 yard line to give Farmersville the short field. The drive concluded when Bobby Bishop ran it in from a yard out for the Farmers' second touchdown, then he connected with Kevin Shinn for the two-point conversion to put the Farmers up, 14-0.

The Wylie offense, meanwhile, was stalling.

Rock King took over for Ronnie Cross at quarterback in the first quarter after Ronnie landed on his elbow. In the second quarter, the Pirate offense still lagged; early in the second period, Bobby Bishop picked off Rock's pass in the end zone, the first of two interceptions Rock threw on the night. Later in that quarter, Wylie faced a fourth and 10 situation from the Farmer 19 yard line and disdained the field goal attempt in favor of the old hook and ladder play, known to the Pirates as the "flea flicker."

On the fourth down play, Rock drilled a pass to Garth Touchstone, who caught the ball and lateraled to Wayne Mayberry, who raced up the left sideline for the Pirate touchdown. Rickey Blackman's point after attempt was wide right, however, and the Farmers held an eight point lead at 14-6.

According to Rock, the Pirates practiced this flea flicker play a great deal, but seldom utilized it in game situations. Tom Landry, former coach of the Dallas

Cowboys, invented the play in the 1960s. The tight end was running a regular route, with the only difference being the running back was trailing the play in the flat instead of staying in the backfield to block. The tight end, upon catching the ball, actually had the option to pitch the ball or to keep it and run—though he would have had to make up his mind fairly quickly, since his back was to the defender off of which he was "optioning."

Whatever the circumstances, the trio of Rock, Garth and Wayne made this play work—and later the coaching staff would call for this play again in a key situation in the 1977 playoffs with three different players.

On the Pirates' first possession of the second half, after a Farmersville punt, they drove 74 yards behind the running of Wayne Mayberry and Wendell Collins. At one point, Wayne kept the drive going with a crucial four-yard run on a fourth and one play to the Farmer 18 yard line.

After Rock hit Doug Gollahon for an 11-yard gain, Wayne Mayberry plowed in from seven yards out for the touchdown. The Pirates went for two in an attempt to tie the score, but Rock's pass intended for Garth Touchstone fell incomplete.

Wayne Mayberry led Wylie with 44 yards rushing on 10 attempts for the game, but it was Wayne Tyson who took control on the Pirates' next possession, gaining most of the yardage on a lengthy Wylie drive. The Pirates lost yardage, however, when on a second down pitchout, Farmersville read the play perfectly and forced Wylie into a third and 19. The drive stalled.

The Pirate defense did not allow Farmersville into the end zone after the first quarter, but the Farmer defense was equal to the task. In the fourth quarter, Farmersville began to win the field position game with the help of Elvin Taylor's booming punts. The Pirates started their first possession of the final quarter with good field position on their own 40, but Rock fumbled the ball and Elvin Taylor was there to recover for the Farmers.

Elvin's punts forced Wylie to start from their own seven, 11 and 13 yard line on their final three possessions, and it proved too much for the Pirates to overcome.

"That was very big," Bobby Bishop said of Elvin's punts. "That game was totally about field position."

Wylie out gained the Farmers in total yardage (272 to 226) and gained more first downs (14 to 8), but turnovers hurt the Pirates. Wylie turned the ball over to the Farmers four times (two fumbles and two interceptions) compared to just one turnover for Farmersville to give the Farmers a plus three ratio in that category.

The contest with Farmersville was mostly a defensive battle. Wylie had kept the Farmers out of the end zone after the first quarter, and the Farmers had answered the call to hang on to the slim lead after the offense did all the team's scoring in the first 10 minutes.

"Defensively, (Wylie) was very tough," Bobby Bishop remembered. "I was very beat up after that game."

The Farmers had avenged the previous year's defeat. Meanwhile, however, the Pirates, who began the season ranked in the state's top 10 by the Associated Press, were 1-2 in their first three games. They had just lost to a team that competed in a lower classification.

"That was a very disappointing loss," Rock said of the Farmersville game. "We felt like after the Kaufman game, although we got beat physically and on the scoreboard, we played a good hard game and executed things well. The Farmersville game, we didn't execute things very well. We did some things, and turned the ball over some and just did not play well."

Perhaps most important, the Farmersville game gave the Wylie players and coaches a much better indicator for the Pirates' season than either of the first two games did. And, as all non-district games do, it gave the Pirates a chance to experiment. As a case in point, with the Pirates pinned deep in their own territory, Coach Shaffer called for a counter-option play that featured a "crackback block," which had just been declared illegal by the UIL. The Pirates were penalized for the block and a big gain was nullified—one that could have potentially been a momentum turner against Farmersville.

"We knew we had a good football team by that time," Coach Shaffer said. "We were beginning to find out what we could and couldn't do. And we found out the style of play that we could use. We found out that we couldn't crackback anymore. We couldn't even afford to take that chance, so we stopped that forever. We never, ever ran another play that had a crackback block in the scheme."

According to receivers coach Bruce King, the muddy conditions at Farmer Stadium were a hindrance to Wylie's passing game, which they relied on so heavily for the team to be successful.

"I feel like we should not have lost that ballgame," Coach King explained. "It was just muddy and sloppy, and it really made it almost impossible for us to throw the ball and play the kind of ball that we needed to."

The first three games did not count toward the standings, but if the Pirates were going to repeat as district champions, something needed to change and fast. They needed to eliminate the mistakes they had made against Kaufman and Farmersville.

"I don't think we played that badly in the two losses," Doug Gollahon recalled. "We played a couple of pretty good teams. We needed to make some adjustments. I think from that point on, we were just determined that we weren't going to lose another game."

The loss to Farmersville in week three provided a wakeup call to nearly everyone in the Wylie football camp. Farmersville was a rival and had a strong team, but also had a much smaller enrollment than Wylie High School and was generally considered to be beatable by everyone in Wylie.

Hence, following that loss to Farmersville, Coach Shaffer gave his team a rather memorable pep talk that to this day stands out in the kids' minds.

If the Pirates were unsure of themselves after starting the season at 1-2, their head coach was not. According to Ronnie Cross, "I'll never forget Coach Shaffer coming in after that ballgame and telling us, 'We ain't losing another one.' We kind of didn't know how to take that. I don't know if he was really serious when he said it, but he said it, and I'll be dadgummed if we didn't lose another one from there on out."

At least one of the Pirates knew how to take it. Phil Lemons said of Coach Shaffer's statement, "I believed him. He was just short of God. If he said something, it usually happened."

According to Rock King, "It's ironic, but it was actually prophetic. I'm sure he had no intention of saying that we wouldn't lose another game and win the state championship, because we were a long way from that, at that point, as a team."

Rickey Blackman recalled the mood of the team after the loss to Farmersville: "I knew we were all disappointed, obviously, that we had failed to play up to the level that we should have been playing. What stands out in my mind is that Coach Shaffer came in after that game, and we were all just quiet. We were a very well-disciplined team anyway, so there wasn't going to be any acting up.

"Coach Shaffer came in and told us we weren't through, that things were looking up, and he had the right people in the right places," Rickey continued. "I can't remember the exact quote, but he basically said he knew we weren't gonna lose a game for the rest of the year. I know that really stood out in my mind for him to come in and tell us that. He was basically predicting that we had it on track, and we were gonna do the right things and we were gonna start winning. At 1-2, for him to come in and make a statement like that really stood out in my mind. Of course, he ended up being right all the way to state."

Bob Skipwith remembered of Coach Shaffer's declaration following the Farmersville game: "I don't know if it was more of a threat, or how he meant it. I remember pretty vividly we were sitting up in some bleachers in a gym that we were using as a locker room, and we had just lost the game, and he came out and said, 'We're not gonna lose again.' I recall Jess Croley turning to some of the guys up there and mumbling under his breath, 'What does he think we're gonna do, win state?'"

Jess's comment caused a dull roar among the team members, which the coaches immediately quieted. Looking back, Jess recalled what prompted the remark—it was the simple fact that on paper, the prospect of this Pirate team going undefeated for the rest of the 1977 season seemed highly unlikely.

"The way we had played the last two games, I thought, man, it's gonna be a long season," Jess explained. "I thought we might be successful and have a winning program, but in my mind, at that point, there was no way we would go undefeated the rest of the year."

By declaring the Pirates would not lose again that season, what Shaffer had done was issue a challenge to his team. And they responded on the field, as their play in the next 12 games indicated.

"That loss," Roy Fuentes explained, "really was a key part of bringing everybody together and making everybody focus."

"We were 1-2 at that point, and knew that we really had a long way to go," Coach Bruce King said. "We certainly weren't thinking about a state championship, necessarily, or even a district championship. We were thinking, 'What can we do to win next week?'"

Coach Page remembered, "The kids just never gave up hope…I think the kids still believed in and bought into the idea that things were going to turn around. We went up the next week against Justin Northwest, got a bunch of turnovers and played well, and it just began to snowball from there."

Indeed, the snowball started rolling the following week with Justin Northwest, which proved to be just the tonic the Pirates needed to get back on track.

Game Four, Wylie vs. Justin Northwest

Playing their final non-district game of the season September 23, the Pirates handled the Justin Northwest Texans at Pirate Stadium much the way they did Fort Worth Diamond Hill on opening night—the defense forced turnovers and the offense turned those takeaways into points. And this was against a Justin Northwest team that had beaten the Pirates, 9-6, in the fourth game of 1976.

One thing that gave the Pirates a much-needed lift for the rematch with Northwest was the official return of senior strong safety Tony Garner, who missed most of the first three games with a pulled groin muscle. As part of his injury rehabilitation, Tony drove 10 miles southwest of Wylie to Garland for physical therapy every day during a study hall period for about a week and a half at the start of the season.

Tony had an outstanding game defensively against the Texans, coming down with two of the Pirates' three interceptions. The Pirates also forced a fumble that was key, giving them four turnovers on the evening in the 30-0 Wylie victory. What makes Tony's stats for that game all the more amazing is that he played only about half the game, since the coaches were easing him back into the lineup due to the groin injury.

"We missed him quite a bit," free safety Wayne Mayberry said of Tony, his partner in the defensive secondary. "Wherever the ball was, there he was."

One of Tony's personal goals was to top his 19 interceptions which he compiled in 1976. After playing Justin Northwest in 1977, Tony needed only 17 picks to tie his remarkable interception total from the year before.

Ronnie started at quarterback and rotated with Rock throughout the game. But Rock had his biggest impact of the evening as the Pirates' punter. He played the same role against Northwest that Elvin Taylor played so well for Farmersville the week before against the Pirates. Rock averaged an amazing 49 yards per punt—one of which covered 69 yards—thus pinning Northwest deep in their own territory for much of the evening and allowing Wylie to win the field position game.

"Rock King was a weapon," Jack Hirmon remembered. "The guy could kick a 42-yard punt in a spiral with huge hang time on it. Even if we got stopped, we could pin the opposing team way back in their own zone, because he had a cannon for a leg."

The Pirate defense played an outstanding game, limiting the Texan running game to 42 yards and the passing attack to 116 yards for a total of just 158 yards of offense.

"The coaches always got us up and ready to play against our next opponent," Rock recalled, "and Northwest was somebody that we felt like we should play well against if we do what we should. Our defense, in my opinion, carried the team that year. You know that old adage, 'Defense wins championships, offense wins games'—I think that's true. They certainly stepped up and had a good game against Northwest."

The two teams played to a scoreless tie after 12 minutes; then in the second period, the Wylie offense went to work.

The Texans fumbled the ball early in the second quarter and Wylie recovered at the Northwest 25. On the Pirates' first play of the ensuing drive, Wayne Mayberry ran 25 yards to paydirt. Rock King, now handling the placekicking duties, nailed the extra point for a 7-0 Wylie lead.

With two minutes left in the first half, Rock connected with Garth Touchstone for an apparent touchdown, but it was nullified by a holding penalty. The drive ended with a 31-yard field goal from Rock with 30 seconds left in the first half, and the Pirates carried a 10-0 advantage to the locker room.

To begin the second half, the Wylie offense faced a strong wind; therefore, for the most part, they scrapped their passing game in favor of the run. In the third quarter, the Pirates marched 81 yards, mostly via the ground game, and capped the drive with a five-yard touchdown run by Dale Morgan. Rock kicked the extra point, but it was called back due to a holding penalty, and his second attempt was no good. Still, the Pirates led, 16-0, and the way the Pirate defense was playing, it might as well have been 160-0 for Northwest.

Three minutes later, Wayne Tyson joined the scoring parade with a seven-yard touchdown run, and Rock added the PAT for a 23-0 Wylie lead. Then, with seven minutes left in the game, Rock found Garth Touchstone from a yard out, and this time it counted. Rock's point after provided the final margin.

First on the list of District 12-2A opponents was Cedar Hill. The Pirates evened their record at 2-2 and played a near flawless game on offense, defense and special teams against Justin Northwest. If they were going to repeat as district champions, they needed that Cedar Hill game to start things off.

Game Five, Wylie vs. Cedar Hill

On September 30, the Pirates played their second consecutive home game, and this one counted in the standings. The first District 12-2A opponent of 1977 was the Cedar Hill Longhorns, who won three out of four non-district games going into the matchup with Wylie.

The Pirates turned in an "unartistic" effort on offense, as deemed by Coach Shaffer in one of the local newspapers. The Pirates' effort was unartistic, if not downright sloppy; Wylie turned the ball over five times (three on fumbles, two on interceptions), and three of those gave the Longhorns good field position with which to work. But Northwest could not do anything with their field position on this particular night due to the repeated heroic stands of the Wylie defense. The Longhorns scored their only touchdown of the evening on special teams.

The Pirate defense came through time and time again against the Longhorns, led by defensive tackle Chuck Edge, whose ability to read keys by the Cedar Hill offensive line consistently tipped him off as to which play was running and allowed him to thwart it.

"He could see it all," Coach Shaffer said of his defensive tackle. "He had the greatest vision and recognition ability of any player I've ever coached. As a result, that made him a special defensive player. As an offensive player, he was a good one, but nothing like he was on defense."

Coach Rick Page, the Pirates' defensive coordinator, said of Chuck, "In all my time in the business, 32 years, this young man played two technique (the interior defensive line position) better than anybody that I've ever coached. He just had a knack for it. He had a great ability to what we called 'pop the tail,' which at the moment of contact was to extend out and deliver a blow into the guy. It kept those big linemen that were always blocking on him off of him."

Though the Pirates defense allowed Cedar Hill 300 total yards (243 of which came on the ground), the Longhorns had trouble mounting a sustained drive. The linebacker trio of Garth Touchstone, Rickey Blackman and Mark Whitehead made sure of that. The Cedar Hill offense did not reach the end zone; the Longhorns scored their only six-pointer of the night on a kickoff return.

The Wylie turnovers may have given Cedar Hill the short field, but Rock King's punts once again kept them back for much of the evening. Rock punted the ball five times for a 51-yard average against Cedar Hill.

The two teams ended the first quarter deadlocked in a scoreless tie, and the Pirates drew first blood in the second quarter with a 68-yard drive. All of those 68 yards came on the ground.

The key play to keep the drive going was a 20-yard run by Dale Morgan. Once the Pirates reached the two, Wayne Tyson bowled over the goal line for the Wylie touchdown with 3:20 left in the first half. Rock kicked the extra point, but an offsides penalty on Cedar Hill gave the Pirates another shot, and the second time (from a yard and a half closer), they elected to go for two. Wayne Tyson's run was true, and the Pirates took an 8-0 lead over Cedar Hill into the intermission.

The defenses ruled again in the third quarter, as neither team could score in the stanza. In the fourth quarter, standing 80 yards from the opponent's end zone, Rock completed a short pass to Doug Gollahon, who broke a couple of tackles on the way to running the length of the field for the score. Doug caught only two passes on the evening but they were both huge, covering a total of 105 yards. Rock booted the extra point after Doug's touchdown for a 15-0 Pirate lead.

Cedar Hill caught its only break of the night on the ensuing kickoff when Howard Verdell returned it 85 yards for a Longhorn touchdown. But they could not get any closer to Wylie than nine points.

The Pirates were now halfway through the regular season and had taken a giant step toward defending the District 12-2A crown with the win over Cedar Hill.

The Midlothian Panthers, who were undefeated and coming off a bye week, were the next obstacle. They were thought of by many to be serious challengers for the 12-2A title. By many outside of Wylie, that is.

Game Six, Wylie vs. Midlothian

In order to knock off the team many thought was Wylie's toughest district opponent, the Pirate defense would need a repeat performance of the Cedar Hill game. They got exactly that.

The rains pelted the field in Midlothian as the Pirates took on the Panthers on the night of October 7. All the Pirate defense did was repeatedly kill Panther drives with takeaways—five of them, to be exact—and hold them to six points in a 23-6 drubbing.

The Midlothian offense fumbled the ball away to Wylie four times (Danny Schultz, Chuck Edge, Jess Croley and Rickey Blackman each had a fumble recovery for the Pirates) and threw one interception. The one pick went to Tony Garner, his fifth of the season—despite missing most of the first three games with a pulled muscle.

The quarterback position was still somewhat unsettled at the time the Midlothian game began. Ronnie Cross, the senior, had started all the games to that point and had played most of the snaps in the first three contests of the season. Starting with Justin Northwest in the fourth game, Rock King began to rotate in at quarterback a little more frequently.

Ronnie started against Midlothian, but Coach Shaffer replaced him with Rock after the Pirates' first possession and Rock played the rest of the game under center. But despite playing most of the game against Midlothian, Rock never considered himself to be the Pirates' No. 1 signal caller; he just figured he would continue getting chances to play if he worked hard.

"There wasn't a specific time where I felt like I've got to be the guy," Rock said. "During that game, I subbed in, and Ronnie had started the game and I finished the game—which was a little unusual, because even in the games that we split, we would interchange series almost at times. It wasn't a situation where one of us went in and played the rest of the game out. I think some of it may have been dictated by the defense, and how much we were gonna run, or how much we were gonna pass.

"We just both continued working, and we felt like we both would get an opportunity to play some."

The Wylie offense did not commit a single turnover, despite the rain. The defense had come to play, but it took the Pirate offense a while to get rolling—the first half ended in a scoreless tie.

It did not take long in the second half for Wylie to make a move. Dale Morgan returned the Panthers' second-half kickoff 70 yards to the Midlothian 17 yard line. The return resulted in the game's first points, which came in the form of a 28-yard Rock King field goal with 10:03 left in the third quarter.

The Panthers began their next drive, but it ended suddenly in Pirate territory when Tony Garner knocked the ball loose from Midlothian's Norman Lampkins. Danny Schultz recovered the fumble for Wylie. The impact of the hit on Norman knocked Tony unconscious.

"Norman held some of the sprint records for the district," Tony described. "He was just lightning fast. I always played strong safety, and he turned the corner about the time I got there. The next thing I know, I remember somebody waking me up…we both kind of got knocked down and laid there a while and got up. It must have been (a hard hit) to put us both on the ground. I remember turning the corner and him clearing the hole about the same time I did. Odds are, if you looked at the films, neither one of us probably ever saw the other one coming, would be my guess."

The Pirates padded their lead later in the third quarter when Rock found Doug Gollahon for an 18-yard touchdown pass. After the extra point attempt failed, the Pirates led, 9-0, with 5:22 remaining in the third quarter.

Late in the third period, a Rock King punt pinned the Panthers on their own five yard line. A delay of game penalty backed them up to the two and a half, and on the next play, they fumbled and Rickey Blackman recovered in the end zone for Wylie.

"We had 'em down on the goal line," Rickey remembered. "It was still a pretty close game at the time, and we ran one of our gap defensive blitzes that we ran were I came down and played tackle instead of linebacker. I think that was the first time we'd run it all year. We ran the blitz and I came in and hit the quarterback and made him fumble, and we scored a touchdown on that."

After the fumble recovery for the touchdown, Rock kicked the extra point to increase Wylie's lead to 16-0.

In the fourth quarter, Pirate defensive tackle Chuck Edge recovered yet another Midlothian fumble. As was their custom, Wylie turned this takeaway into a touchdown—a three-yard strike from Rock to Tony Garner, who was back in the game after having the wind knocked out in the third quarter. The Wylie lead swelled to 23-0 after Rock kicked the PAT.

Harlan Whitlock provided a too-little, too-late touchdown for Midlothian in the fourth quarter after a blocked punt set up the Panthers at the Wylie five. The kick failed, making the score 23-6, which was the eventual final.

The Pirates had now hit their stride, and they were playing their best football of the season—particularly on the defensive side of the ball—heading into the bye week on October 14. The Pirate defense had allowed only six points in two district games, and those six points came after a five-yard drive. The Pirates had yet to allow the opponent's offense a sustained drive in district play.

With several players banged up, the Pirates now had a week off before heading home to renew the old Collin County rivalry with the Allen Eagles on homecoming night.

Game Seven, Wylie vs. Allen

The Pirates returned home for the Allen game following the bye week sporting a 2-0 district record (4-2 overall). They had not lost a district game in two years and seemed to be catching all the breaks since the two-point loss to Farmersville in the season's third game.

The season had gone the opposite way for the Allen Eagles, however. They came into the Wylie game October 21 having lost five of seven on the season—three of those losses came by the slimmest of margins—and the Eagles had yet to win a district game in three tries.

Nevertheless, Allen, which sat down the road just north of Plano, had proven a worthy opponent for the Pirates over the years. They were not to be taken lightly. They wanted to knock the Pirates off on Wylie's homecoming night.

In the end, the Pirate machine proved too much for Allen to stop, and Wylie walked away 37-10 winners over the Eagles.

The Pirates jumped out to a 6-0 lead over the Eagles in the first quarter with a 43-yard touchdown drive, ending with an 11-yard run by Wendell Collins. On that drive, Wayne Tyson contributed a 15-yard run and Rock King, who drew his first start of the season at quarterback, added a seven-yard scramble.

On the second play of the ensuing Allen drive, Greg Duncan fumbled and Roy Fuentes pounced on the loose ball for Wylie on the Allen 18. The Eagles turned the ball over four times on the night compared to three for the Pirates.

This particular turnover did not cost Allen a touchdown, but the Pirates came away with three on a 35-yard field goal by Rock King to give them a 9-0 lead.

Allen answered with 10 second-quarter points, beginning with a 16-yard touchdown pass from Steve Marion to Greg Duncan, after which Zenford Jones kicked the extra point. The short runs of David Grimes, who was Allen's top rusher in the game with 67 yards on 17 attempts, helped to sustain the drive.

The Eagles controlled the clock in the second period, owning the ball for almost 10 minutes out of 12. Their next drive after the touchdown resulted in a 31-yard field goal by Zenford Jones with 2:09 left in the first half. Zenford's field goal gave Allen a 10-9 lead, marking the first time Wylie trailed since the Farmersville game more than a month earlier.

Coach Shaffer was faced with a decision with two minutes to work with. Was he going to concede the first half and be satisfied with his team down by a point with 24 minutes left to play? Or was he going to use what time he had to try and regain the lead for Wylie before the intermission, despite facing a strong south wind?

He made his decision, and the Pirates responded with an eight-play, 70-yard touchdown drive that took less than a minute. Rock King made a key scramble on the scoring drive for 15 yards and completed four passes into the wind, including one to Doug Gollahon for a 16-yard gain on third and one. The Pirates were also helped out by a 15-yard personal foul penalty on the Eagles.

An eight-yard touchdown strike from Rock to Garth Touchstone capped the drive, and Rock's PAT gave Wylie a 16-10 lead heading into halftime. Coach Shaffer later called that drive the turning point in the game.

According to Rock, the hurry-up, two-minute offense was something that the Pirates were not used to running in game situations. The Houston veer offense was not conducive to large gains.

"I remember (Shaffer) calling consecutive plays, and that's something that was unusual," Rock said. "He normally hand-signaled everything in, but I know when we called timeout at the change of possession, he said we're going to run this, and this, and this, and make sure you get out of bounds, and make sure if you don't get out of bounds, you get a timeout. He managed the clock and told us what to do prior to it. It was a big drive for us, and we ended up scoring."

In the third quarter, the Eagles had an excellent chance to take the lead when Zenford Jones picked off a Rock King pass and returned it to the Wylie 38. The Pirate defense held, however, to maintain the Pirates' slim six-point advantage.

Early in the fourth quarter, the Pirates had a golden opportunity to add to their six-point lead stolen right out of their hands—literally. After Garth Touchstone intercepted Allen quarterback Steve Marion and returned the ball to the Eagle 25, Wayne Tyson bulldozed through for 15 yards to the 10. On a third and eight play, Rock appeared to complete the pass to Doug Gollahon in the end zone, but Doug found himself locked in a struggle for the ball with Allen defensive back Sandy Bedell. Somehow, Sandy managed to pry the ball loose from Doug to give the Eagles the touchback.

The game remained close until the Wylie pulled away midway through the fourth quarter, after Ronnie Cross entered the game at quarterback for the Pirates. A short Allen punt gave the Pirates the ball on the Eagle 45 yard line, and Wayne Mayberry ran the ball up the middle on the first play of the drive. The Eagles appeared to have Wayne stopped for a short gain, but somehow he broke loose and went all the way for the touchdown. In one of the local newspapers, Allen coach John Pearce later called Wayne's touchdown run the turning point.

"We all hit at one time, and everybody just let go of me," Wayne remembered of his crucial touchdown play against Allen. "I mean, they had me. I could feel 'em hitting me everywhere, and then all of a sudden, I'm five yards away and there's nobody in sight…it was the weirdest thing I've ever seen."

Ronnie Cross provided more fireworks with a 32-yard touchdown run, and Rock's extra point put the Pirates up by 20 points at 30-10. But the Pirates were not done yet.

On Allen's next possession, Tony Garner came down with his second interception of the game and seventh of the season. Tony's pick on a pass intended for Zenford Jones gave the Pirates the ball on their own 35.

"He was doing a streak route, and I came across and just pulled one out of his hands," Tony explained. "That one kind of meant something because the previous year, my junior year, I got beat in Allen for a touchdown. You always kind of look back going, okay, they owe me one."

On Wylie's ensuing drive, Wayne Mayberry got the call to run the ball and appeared to be off to the races when he was caught from behind by Zenford Jones, who was still giving it his all despite the fact that Allen trailed by three touchdowns late in the fourth quarter. As it was, Wayne gained 30 yards on the play.

The drive ended with Ronnie's second touchdown of the game, this time on a two-yard plunge, with just 43 seconds remaining. Rock's PAT provided the exclamation point and the 37-10 final.

The Pirates dominated in total offensive yardage over Allen (327 to 164). Wylie gained 284 yards on the ground, led by Wayne Mayberry's 85 yards on four attempts. Rock's punting was again well above average; this time the sophomore averaged 41 yards over five punts.

Wylie was now 4-0 in district play (5-2 on the season) and ready to head south on Interstate 35 to take on the Red Oak Hawks on Red Oak's homecoming night.

Game Eight, Wylie vs. Red Oak

Perhaps Chuck Edge summed this game up best when he said, "It was ugly."

It really depends on whose side you were on. It was ugly if you were a Red Oak fan. But if you rooted for Wylie, this was the kind of game you needed every now and then.

On October 28, the Pirates came out with all guns blazing against the Hawks on Red Oak's homecoming night. What resulted was an easy 52-0 Wylie victory.

It took a while for the Pirate offense to find a groove, but once they did, they scored often. In fact, they scored so often that Rock King had to punt only once, and it went for 43 yards. Wylie outgained the Hawks in first downs (19 to 11) and more than doubled their total offensive yards (426 to 179). With the veer offense, the Pirates gained 338 yards on the ground against the hapless Hawk defense.

Even third-string quarterback Bruce "Doc" Cryer got in on the touchdown action, crossing the end zone twice in the fourth quarter with the outcome already decided.

Despite the touchdown barrage, Wylie actually did not score until the second period because they were trying to figure out the defense that Red Oak was running.

The Hawks' defensive scheme worked for about a quarter and a half. Then the flood gates opened.

Ronnie Cross started at quarterback for Wylie. He put the Pirates on the board first with a 52-yard touchdown run on an option play about halfway through the second quarter, and the Pirates led, 7-0, after Rock's extra point. Rock kicked a 32-yard field goal with 42 seconds left in the first half to make it 10-0, Pirates.

Still, this was Red Oak, and in the mind of the Pirates' coaching staff, their team should have been ahead by more than 10 points at halftime.

"We had played two or three really good games in a row, and I think going into Red Oak, we were a little overconfident, and we probably didn't prepare as well as we should have, emotionally, for the game," Rock King explained. "And

Game Eight, Wylie vs. Red Oak 55

they did throw some wrinkles at us on defense, and we didn't make good adjustments. Not until halftime."

The Pirates made some adjustments at halftime, according to Rock—some with Xs and Os and some psychological. "I remember it being a pretty lively halftime for the coaches and the players," he said.

In the second half, the Pirate offense turned on the afterburners. On their first play from scrimmage in that half, Wayne Mayberry raced 52 yards for the touchdown and Rock kicked the extra point to put the Pirates up, 17-0. Later in the third, Doug Gollahon ran 48 yards for a touchdown after grabbing a short pass up the middle from Rock, and the rout was on.

Wendell Collins tacked on yet another Pirate touchdown late in the third period with a 50-yard run.

The Pirates were still not finished scoring by the time the fourth quarter rolled around. They continued to pour it on, capping a 60-yard drive with a nine-yard touchdown run from Wayne Mayberry. On the ensuing Red Oak drive, Dan Whitt picked off a pass and returned it 35 yards to the Hawk two yard line. Bruce Cryer, who had taken over at quarterback for the Pirates, scored on the keeper just moments later. By this time, backup place-kicker Kevin Adams was in the game attempting the extra points for the Pirates.

The option play provided the final touchdown of the evening for Wylie, which came in the form of a 19-yard run by Bruce Cryer. A bad snap spoiled Kevin's PAT attempt, but holder Ronnie Cross recovered to complete a pass to Wayne Tyson for the two-point conversion to make it 52-0.

The Pirates knew that in 1977, the Red Oak Hawks were one of the weaker teams in District 12-2A and had been for many years. In fact, Red Oak was in the 37th year of a 42-year playoff drought in 1977 (that drought ended in 1982 under the leadership of Head Coach Rick Page, who took that position in 1981).

"In Red Oak (in 1977), you play the game, get it overwith, hope nobody gets hurt, then you get ready to start the next game," Coach Shaffer explained. "You've got to take them seriously. You get all the points on the board that you're going to need to win, then you start playing a lot of other players."

On the same Friday night that Wylie was routing the Red Oak Hawks, Midlothian was taking care of another challenger for the district crown, Forney. Still, the Wylie-Forney matchup loomed large on the horizon for many in the Pirate football camps. With a 4-0 district mark, the Pirates could clinch a share of the District 12-2A crown with a win over their old foes, the Forney Jackrabbits.

Game Nine, Wylie vs. Forney

Much was riding on this game, played out November 4 at Pirate Stadium, for both sides. Wylie could clinch a share of the district title with a win. The Forney Jackrabbits were still in the running for the 12-2A crown and no doubt were still stinging from that loss to Wylie three years earlier—on their home turf in Forney—that cost them the district title.

"They were about the same as we were," Wayne Mayberry recalled. "They didn't have very many people that actually had any size to 'em. We both played about the same. I think they probably had a little better speed. It was pretty close."

As it turned out, it *was* pretty close, but the Pirates' defense held off the charging Jackrabbits in the ninth game of the 1977 season. The play of quarterback Rock King was key as well in a 17-14 win that guaranteed Wylie a tie for the district crown.

This game was memorable in particular to one of the Pirates, Tony Garner, not just because Wylie grabbed a share of the district title, but because it was the last game he played against one of Forney's stars, Antyonne Ashley. Like Tony did for the Pirates, Antyonne played flanker and strong safety for the Jackrabbits and the two had somewhat of an individual rivalry going on throughout their high school football careers.

Coach Shaffer started senior Ronnie Cross at quarterback, and the game began inauspiciously for him—Forney defensive back Paul Alexander intercepted his pass in the first quarter and returned it to the Wylie 21. The turnover led to the first score of the game, an 18-yard touchdown strike from Forney quarterback Billy Pringle to Gibby House. Chuck Edge charged through and blocked Antyonne Ashley's extra-point attempt, but still, Wylie was in an unfamiliar position, trailing 6-0. It was only the second time in the previous six games the Pirates had trailed, and the other time was by a point only briefly against Allen two weeks earlier.

A punt gave the Pirates the ball on their own 24 in the waning moments of the first quarter. Then Rock King entered the game at quarterback for Wylie.

On the last play of the first quarter, Forney's Mike Wittenburg sacked Rock for a six-yard loss. But a facemask penalty on Forney nullified the play, and Wylie had new life. Rock made key completions to Garth Touchstone (15 yards) and Wendell Collins (18 yards) on the drive before Wendell darted 20 yards though the right side for the touchdown. Rock's extra point gave the Pirates a one-point lead at 7-6.

Later in the second quarter, Forney's John Cates recovered Wayne Tyson's fumble at the Jackrabbit 25. But the Jackrabbits came up empty on the drive when the Pirate defense stopped Paul Alexander on a fourth and two play from the seven.

On their next possession, the Jackrabbits were presented another golden opportunity to grab the lead when Chris Couch raced 58 yards to the Wylie 11. The Jackrabbits were unable to move the ball, however, and they settled for a 27-yard field goal attempt. But the snap was high, the kick was no good and Forney came away empty once more.

The inability of the Jackrabbits to come away with points on either of those two drives proved to be extremely costly, as the final margin indicated.

On their first possession of the second half, Rock and the Pirates made something happen. Wylie marched 65 yards to pad their lead, helped out by a crucial 19-yard run from Wayne Mayberry on third and two and a 15-yard completion from Rock to Roy McClendon. The drive ended when Rock completed an 18-yard pass play to Doug Gollahon, who smashed his way past two Forney defenders to cross the goal line. After Rock kicked the extra point, the Pirates led, 14-6, with five minutes left to play in the third period.

"Doug had a huge game that game," Rock recalled. "He made some big plays. He broke tackles on little short routes that would have otherwise been five or six yard gains, and he turned them into touchdowns...Doug had a lot of outstanding games, but I particularly remember him shining in that game."

With nine minutes remaining in the game, Rock booted a 41-yard field goal—his longest of the season to date—to give Wylie a 17-6 cushion.

Forney did not simply roll over, however. They mounted a sustained drive helped out by two huge Wylie penalties, one a defensive holding infraction and the other a pass interference play in the end zone. Paul Alexander scored from two yards out and Chris Couch, Forney's leading rusher for the game with 95 yards on 13 carries, ran around the left end for the two-point conversion to pull the Jackrabbits to within three at 17-14 with just under seven minutes remaining.

The Jackrabbits needed the ball back to complete their comeback attempt, but the Pirates made sure they never got that chance. Rock King methodically moved the Pirates down the field to control the clock and keep the Forney offense off the field.

The drive began with a tough 14-yard run by Wayne Mayberry. A few plays later, on third and nine, Rock completed a pass to Garth Touchstone for a 10-yard gain with five minutes left to play. Then, with 1:42 remaining and the Pirates looking at a fourth and five from the Forney 30 yard line, Coach Shaffer had a decision to make.

Rock's longest field goal of the season to that point was 41 yards, achieved earlier in that game; this attempt would be 47 yards. A field goal would not put the game out of reach, however; it would give Wylie only a six-point lead, and Forney could still win with a touchdown.

If the Pirates were going to put the game away then and there, they needed a first down. Coach Shaffer was confident the way his defense was playing that Forney would not be able to march the length of the field against them in less than two minutes with no time outs even if the Jackrabbits were to get the ball back.

The Pirates went for it, and it worked. Rock found Doug Gollahon for a seven-yard gain to the 23 for the first down, and the Pirates were able to run the clock out. It did not come easy—Doug had to make a one-handed grab on Rock's pass, which was not as accurate as Rock had hoped it would be.

"The play was 23, where the tight end takes about three steps and goes into the flat," Rock described. "He was wide open, and I threw it way low and to his outside. I remember him diving, and he one-handed the ball. It was one of those (catches) where it just stuck in his hand. We ended up getting a first down, we kept the ball and were able to run the clock out."

Wylie won despite committing 12 penalties accounting for 114 lost yards. Wayne Mayberry was again the team's leading rusher for the game with 63 yards on nine attempts, and Wendell Collins was close behind with 53 yards on 12 carries.

A share of the District 12-2A title belonged to Wylie. The win over Forney was the Pirates' sixth in a row overall and their 11th consecutive win in district play.

"When we were able to beat Forney in that ballgame, it really put us in the driver's seat district-wise," Coach Bruce King explained. "That was just a big win. It wasn't a surprising one, necessarily, but it was one I don't think that anybody that night after the Forney game or the next day when they watched film would have anticipated that we would go through the district undefeated and be district champions at that point. But we certainly were gaining confidence, not only as a coaching staff, but as a team. The players knew they were getting better."

"You have a good, solid high school football team that can play you down to the wire," Coach Shaffer said of the Pirates. "We did not have an overpowering football team. It never became an overpowering football team. It was a finesse football team, offensively and defensively. That's the only way we could have played it."

They played it that way and did it with success. The Pirates were playing like champions and could win the district title outright with a win in the final regular season game over the Ferris Yellowjackets in Ferris.

Wylie coaches Rick Page, left, and Jerry Shaffer congratulate each other after the Pirates' big win at Forney, 15 November 1974. Coach Shaffer called this game one of the two watershed games for the Pirates during his 14-year coaching tenure at WHS (the other was Breckenridge in the 1977 playoffs). Both Coach Shaffer and Coach Page have pointed to this photograph as a favorite.
(Photo from the 1975 Wylie High School yearbook)

A photograph of the 1977 Wylie Pirates varsity team taken prior to the start of the season. Front row, from left: Coach Jerry Shaffer, 31-Wayne Mayberry, 62-Chuck Edge, 46-Dan Whitt, 3-Wendell Collins, Coach Rick Page; second row, Coach Bruce King, 83-Troy Ripple, 85, Roy Fuentes, 37-Dale Downing, 52-Tim Pelton, 67-Joey Hicks, 25-Wayne Tyson, Coach Dick Matkin; third row, Student Manager- Richard Powell, 48-Ricky Meeks, 80-Jack Hirmon, 79-Paul Adams, 20-Dale Morgan, 49-Doug Gollahon, Coach Ken Ard; fourth row, 9-Ronnie Cross, 35-Tony Garner, 10-Rock King, 78-Danny Gurley, 58-Bob Skipwith, 24-Rickey Blackman; back row, 17-Roy McClendon, 66-Lon Wallace, 63-Danny Schultz, 60-Phil Lemons, 84-Garth Touchstone, 18-Mark Whitehead, 55-Jess Croley
(Photo courtesy of Jerry Shaffer)

Ronnie Cross, a.k.a. "Blood," was not as big as a typical quarterback and was not the fastest kid on the block, but he had a rifle for a right arm and he wanted to win. (Photo courtesy of Sue Ann Harper)

Some of the Wylie Pirate backs and receivers at the start of the 1977 season were, front row, from left, Wayne Mayberry, Troy Ripple, Roy Fuentes, Wendell Collins, Wayne Tyson, Dale Morgan and Jack Hirmon. Back row, Dale Downing, Tony Garner, Roy McClendon, Rickey Blackman, Ronnie Cross and Dan Whitt. (Photo courtesy of Sue Ann Harper)

Four members of the 1977 Pirate defense, shown at the beginning of the 1977 season. From left, Dale Morgan, Tony Garner, Rickey Blackman and Roy Fuentes. (Photo courtesy of Sue Ann Harper)

Some of the Wylie Pirate secondary, linebackers and receivers at the beginning of the 1977 season: Front row, from left, Tony Garner, Roy Fuentes, Dale Downing, Troy Ripple and Jack Hirmon. Back row, Doug Gollahon, Ricky Meeks, Garth Touchstone, Roy McClendon and Mark Whitehead. (Photo courtesy of Sue Ann Harper)

Jerry G. Shaffer was the Wylie Pirates' head football coach from 1974–88. (Photo from the 1978 Wylie High School yearbook)

Game Nine, Wylie vs. Forney 67

The Pirates gather in the gym during a pep rally before one of the 1977 playoff games. (Photo courtesy of Sue Ann Harper)

The Pirates file into the gym for a pep rally the day of one of the football games in 1977. Pictured are Lon Wallace (66), Troy Ripple (number obscured), Jess Croley (55), Paul Adams (79), Bob Skipwith (58) and Wayne Tyson (25, far right). (Photo courtesy of Sue Ann Harper)

Game Nine, Wylie vs. Forney 69

The 1977–78 Wylie High School varsity cheerleaders were, from left, Sherry Lemons, Jacklyn Bostic, Sheri Mayberry, Rhonda McCarley, Phyllis McDonald, Peggy Morgan and Rusty Hale. (Photo from the 1978 Wylie High School yearbook)

Tony Garner celebrates after one of his 23 interceptions he recorded in 1977. He had two against Justin Northwest in the fourth game of the season after missing most of the first three games with an injury. (Photo courtesy of Sue Ann Harper)

Game Nine, Wylie vs. Forney   71

*Zealous Wylie fans cheer on the Pirates at one of the 1977 games, led by, from left, Sue Ann Feagin, Robin Ratcliff and Dianne Clemmons.
(Photo courtesy of Sue Ann Harper)*

BRECKENRIDGE VS WYLIE
CLASS AA REGIONAL CHAMPIONSHIP

FRIDAY, NOVEMBER, 25, 1977

The Wylie-Breckenridge game program

The Pirate defense makes the play on Mount Vernon during the 35-10 win in the state quarterfinal game at Mesquite, 2 December 1977. Pictured are Tony Garner (35), Bruce Cryer (48), Mark Whitehead (18) and Dale Morgan (20). (Photo courtesy of Sue Ann Harper)

CLASS AA CHAMPIONSHIP

WYLIE vs. BELLVILLE

BAYLOR STADIUM, WACO, TEXAS
DECEMBER 17, 1977
2:00 p.m.

The Wylie-Bellville game program

Wylie High School students gather in the hallway one day during the week before the state championship game. Pictured are, from left, Robin Ratcliff, Sue Ann Feagin, Garth Touchstone, Guylyn Richards and Jess Croley.
(Photo courtesy of Sue Ann Harper)

The Pirates break through the sign as they run onto the field at Baylor Stadium in Waco before the state championship game, 17 December 1977. Wayne Mayberry (31) is in front. (Photo from the 1978 Wylie High School yearbook)

Game Nine, Wylie vs. Forney 77

Ronnie Cross fakes a handoff to Wayne Mayberry (31) with Wendell Collins (3) in the backfield during the state championship game against Bellville in Waco, 17 December 1977. Phil Lemons (60) is blocking the Bellville defenders. (Photo from the 1978 Wylie High School yearbook)

The Bellville defense pursues Wendell Collins (3) while Ronnie Cross (background, far left) watches in the state championship game in Waco, 17 December 1977. Wendell gained 58 rushing yards on 20 attempts in that game.
(Photo from the 1978 Wylie High School yearbook)

The scoreboard in the background tells the story for the Wylie Pirates as time winds down in the state championship against Bellville, 17 December 1977. (Photo from the 1978 Wylie High School yearbook)

Linebacker Bruce Cryer (48) greets the enthusiastic Wylie Pirate fans after the team's win over Bellville in the state championship game, 17 December 1977. (Photo from the 1978 Wylie High School yearbook)

Defensive tackle Chuck Edge (62) and Coach Rick Page celebrate together after the Pirates defeated the Bellville Brahmas for the state championship, 17 December 1977. (Photo from the 1978 Wylie High School yearbook)

Wayne Tyson
1959–2002

Kenneth Ard
1946–2003
(Photos from the 1978 Wylie High School Yearbook)

The 1977 UIL Class 2A Texas state championship trophy belongs to the Wylie Pirates.

Game Ten, Wylie vs. Ferris

On November 11 in the final game of the regular season, Wylie and Ferris squared off and combined for 12 turnovers (six by each team) and 205 penalty yards. Wylie still managed to dominate, winning, 34-0, for their third shutout in 10 games and their second in district play.

For the second consecutive year, the Pirates had run the table in district play, going 6-0 in both 1976 and 1977. The victory over Ferris gave the Pirates the 1977 District 12-2A crown outright.

The game was played at Ferris on a field that featured less than favorable conditions, according to some Pirates. Not only was the field in bad shape, but there was very little out of bounds room along the sidelines. If a player went even slightly out of bounds, he would have to deal with a chain link fence that surrounded the field. This caused problems for at least one of the Pirates.

"The field was basically concrete, almost," Tony Garner said. "It was so cracked and rough…I can't remember if I intercepted a pass or caught a pass, but I got hit and went under the chain link fence and it took three other people to lift the chain link fence up while they dragged me out from underneath it."

Senior Ronnie Cross started and played the majority of the game at quarterback. Rock King was banged up after the Forney game, bothered in particular by sore ribs. A few of the other Wylie starters were ailing and were held out of the Ferris game as well, since Ferris was one of the weaker teams in the district that year and Wylie had already clinched a share of the district title.

Junior Kevin Adams handled the place-kicking duties in Rock's place and made four of five extra points.

Given the chance to perform, Ronnie did just that; he rushed for more than 100 yards and two touchdowns and passed for most of Wylie's yards through the air. The Wylie passing game was good on eight of 13 tries—and no interceptions.

Wylie rolled up 382 total yards of offense (260 rushing, 122 passing) and scored all 34 of their points in the first half. Wendell Collins added a 100-yard rushing game and two touchdowns to the Pirate attack.

The Yellowjackets fumbled on just the second play of the game from scrimmage, and Wylie turned that one into a five-yard touchdown run by Ronnie Cross.

A bizarre play resulted in the Pirates' next touchdown. Ronnie was hit and fumbled the ball at midfield, and it was scooped up by a Ferris defensive tackle, who ran it to the Wylie 15 before fumbling. The Pirates recovered the loose ball and drove 85 yards for the touchdown, capped by a five-yard run by Wendell Collins.

With just over six minutes left in the first half, Ronnie raced 20 yards for a touchdown to ice a 55-yard Wylie scoring drive. On the Yellowjackets' next possession, the Pirates recovered a fumble at the Ferris 15. After they moved the ball to the two, Coach Shaffer sent Danny Schultz, who normally played at defensive end, in with the play.

Danny lined up in the backfield and took the handoff from Ronnie, and he plunged in from two yards out for the touchdown. It was Danny's first carry of the season (and it proved to be the last). Kevin Adams followed with the extra point to make it 27-0. It was actually Danny's second touchdown of the season; he scored one in the opening game against Diamond Hill when he recovered Rickey Blackman's fumble in the end zone.

"Even in seventh and eighth grade, they'd put Danny in on short yardage, because for the most part, he couldn't be stopped," Tony Garner said. "You give him a yard and say, 'There's some fame and glory' and Schultz is going to go find the end zone."

Wendell Collins scored the final touchdown of the game late in the first half with a 20-yard run, and the Coach Shaffer called off the dogs for the second half while the Wylie defense preserved the shutout.

Center Bob Skipwith played the entire game and helped hold off a charging Ferris defensive line despite suffering from flu-like symptoms. However, not only did Bob not want to come out of the game, but once the Pirates had the game in hand, he was looking forward to going in on the defensive side. He played at center almost exclusively for the Pirates and rarely received the opportunity to play defense.

"It was just sort of one of those coughing, hacking, flu-type things," Bob remembered. "I probably sounded worse than I felt. We had the game well under control, and coach was moving some people around to give 'em some experience. I came off, and (Shaffer) told me that the next defensive series I could go in as a two technique, which was an interior defensive lineman. He heard me cough a few times and he said, 'No, never mind, you're finished for the night.'"

When all was said and done, the Pirates had allowed their six district opponents only 36 points, an average of just six per game over a six-game period. They had won two of those games by shutout.

The Pirates had pulled it off in a season which began so inauspiciously. After the third game of the season at Farmersville, Wylie was picking up the pieces with a 1-2 record. But after the 10th game, the Pirates were 8-2 and were picking up the district championship trophy.

"If you go to Farmersville and you get beat 14-12, you don't think anything about going to the state championship," said Kenneth Nall, the former Wylie quarterback who attended every game that 1977 season. "We were mad. (Farmersville) wasn't *that* good. They were *pretty* good. It was just a bad game for us. We lost that game and all of a sudden, that team jelled. There was no great athlete, it just all came together—boom, boom, boom."

The Pirates were district champions for the second year in a row and fourth time in their history. Now, they needed to win five games against some of the best teams in Texas to claim the UIL Class 2A state title. But no one was looking ahead that far.

In fact, no one was looking beyond the opening round of the playoffs, where Wylie was slated to take on the Granbury Pirates for the bi-district championship for the second year in a row.

Bi-district Playoff, Wylie vs. Granbury

In a town west of Fort Worth called Weatherford at Kangaroo Stadium on November 18, the 1977 Wylie Pirates began down the playoff road. But they drew a tough assignment for the first round of the postseason in Granbury.

Pirate football games were always well-attended, but the playoff games were even more so, no matter how far away they were played, as evidenced by the attendance at the Wylie playoff games in 1971 and 1976. The bi-district game against Granbury, and the remaining playoff games in 1977, were no exception. In fact, many Pirate players and fans recall seeing people in the stands at playoff games they had not seen for many years.

"When you're in the playoffs, then you start seeing people coming out of the woodwork," Kenneth Nall said.

Wylie was without starting defensive tackle/offensive guard Chuck Edge, one of their key two-way players, who was injured. Add to that the fact that junior tight end/middle linebacker Garth Touchstone suffered a knee injury early in the Granbury contest, and Wylie was without two front-line players for most of the game.

At defensive tackle, sophomore Mike Helm, known to his teammates as "Klink," stepped in to take Chuck's place. Klink continued to play a big role even after Chuck returned to the lineup, starting with the Breckenridge game the week after Granbury.

Actually, Garth's knee injury was a blessing in disguise for the Pirate defense. It led Coach Shaffer to the conclusion that Garth had been miscast as the Pirates' middle linebacker all season, thus giving Bruce "Doc" Cryer a chance to step into that position and shine. Bruce's play at middle linebacker was huge in most, if not all five, of the Pirates' playoff games in 1977, particularly in the regional game against Breckenridge and the state championship against Bellville.

"Probably the most important thing that happened in the Granbury game was Garth Touchstone getting his knee hurt, because it forced us to correct a mistake that I had been making all along at middle linebacker," Coach Shaffer explained.

"And Bruce 'Doc' Cryer becomes our starting middle linebacker. Without Doc Cryer at middle linebacker, we don't beat Breckenridge (the week after Granbury), and we couldn't have won several other games, probably. We found out that Doc Cryer is our middle linebacker because of an injury, not because of any stroke of genius, or any skills of coaching or anything of that sort which you hope would be the case."

Bruce had played sporadically at quarterback during the season as the third-string signal caller, but he preferred playing defense. When he got the call not just to play but to start at the middle linebacker position, he was ready. Having played on offense for most of his life to that point, Bruce wanted to be the hammer and not the nail.

"I was the quarterback all my days from the time leading up to my junior year," Bruce said. "I was tired of getting pounded on. I was ready to play some defense. I was ready to dish it out instead of taking it. I got my opportunity (to play) and I liked it. I liked hitting.

"Touchstone was a lot bigger than I was, but he probably wasn't as mean as I was," Bruce went on. "Garth wasn't that crazy about being on defense. He just didn't like the hitting too much. But he did it because he was a team player. And he did a good job."

Coach Rick Page recalled of Bruce, "Here's a guy that was essentially in a backup role all the time, but he got his reps in practice, paid attention to what he was supposed to be doing, stepped in and just did super the rest of the time."

Cornerback Roy Fuentes explained of the Pirates' defensive situation, "We had an excellent defensive line. They gave everything they had every game. By having them play the way they did, it made it easier for the linebackers and also the secondary…Bruce did a great job. He stepped in and we really didn't miss a beat defensively with him in there versus with Garth in there."

The Granbury Pirates were still smarting from a bi-district playoff defeat at the hands of Wylie, 33-14, at Garland Memorial Stadium the year before. Granbury was a slight underdog for the rematch and was poised for revenge.

"I think everybody was a little bit surprised at how the score turned out that first year (1976)," Rock King said. "We were fortunate, and things went right for us, and we beat 'em pretty handily. We certainly didn't expect it to be that easy, scorewise. We knew they'd be ready to play (in 1977), having seen us the year before. We weren't gonna sneak up on 'em the next year. We knew it would be a tough ballgame."

Coach Shaffer opted to start his senior, Ronnie Cross, at quarterback. Rock King was still bothered a bit by sore ribs and could not play quarterback, though he could still kick and punt.

The game started inauspiciously for Ronnie when Granbury defensive back Gene Sledge picked off a pass on Wylie's first possession and ran it back 35 yards for the touchdown. After Ronnie Myers kicked the PAT, Granbury held a 7-0 advantage halfway through the first quarter.

Wylie began the next drive on its own 41, and Ronnie moved the team downfield until he eventually took it in for the score himself on a one-yard keeper play. Rock missed the PAT, however, and Wylie trailed by a point.

A lesser group of guys might have been discouraged by the missed PAT, but this Wylie team had faced tougher situations than that.

"Those guys were real positive about each other and about the team," Rock recalled. "When somebody made a mistake, or didn't have a good play, or missed the extra point, it was just something where they said, 'We'll be alright. We'll have another chance. We'll go back and be able to make up for it.'"

Wylie missed an opportunity to seize the lead in the second quarter. It started when Rickey Blackman picked off a pass from Granbury quarterback Tommy Holmes and took it to the Granbury 44. Later in the drive, despite facing a first and goal situation from the eight, the Wylie offense could not punch it in. The Granbury defense toughened and stopped them at the one on fourth down.

Next it was the Wylie defense's turn to get tough, and they forced Granbury to punt from their own end zone. It set the Wylie Pirates up with the short field on the Granbury 34.

Wylie got close enough for Rock King to try a 32-yard field goal, which he missed. The sophomore kicker caught a break, however, when Granbury was penalized for jumping offsides on the play. The infraction moved the ball up five yards and gave Rock another shot at the field goal, and this time his kick was true from 27 yards out to give Wylie a 9-7 lead with six seconds left in the first half.

The tide swung in favor of Granbury early in the second half when the rival Pirates recovered a Wendell Collins fumble to set them up with good field position on their own 40. Since Wylie's defense had clamped down on the Granbury running game, Granbury repeatedly went to the air on the ensuing drive. Tommy Holmes connected several times with split end Mark Hayworth, son of Granbury head coach Gerald Hayworth, to move the ball. Holmes finally took it home from a yard out to retake the lead for Granbury. After Ronnie Myers kicked the extra point, Granbury led, 14-9, early in the fourth quarter.

Eventually, Wylie took over on its own 46 yard line with four minutes left to play, still down by five. They needed a touchdown; a field goal would only get them to within two, and they likely would not have time to score twice.

On the first play of the drive, a Granbury defender was penalized for a late hit on Wendell Collins, and the 15-yard walkoff moved the ball to the Granbury 39. Ronnie Cross stayed cool and moved the Pirates down the field, keeping an eye on the clock all the way. Soon, with less than a minute to go, the Pirates found themselves at the Granbury six.

Wylie faced a similar situation earlier in the game and had not been able to get in the end zone. They came away from that second quarter drive empty after turning it over on downs at the Granbury one yard line.

Ronnie Cross made sure that would not happen this time. He eschewed the run in favor of a pass play to his favorite target, tight end Doug Gollahon. After scrambling to get away from the charging Granbury defenders, Ronnie found his man in the corner of the end zone and threw a strike. Doug came down with the ball for the go-ahead touchdown with just 32 ticks left on the clock, and Rock nailed the extra point for a 16-14 Wylie lead.

The Pirates held on the rest of the way to win by that same score, and the bi-district championship was theirs. Perhaps the play that loomed largest for Granbury was the offsides penalty just before the end of the first half that gave Rock a shot to redeem himself after the missed field goal. The late hit on Wylie's game-winning drive certainly played a major role in Granbury's demise as well.

"Going into that ballgame, we felt like we were pretty evenly matched, and that we had a good chance to beat 'em," Coach Bruce King described. "But it was a rematch of the year before. I didn't realize until after the game with Coach (Gerald) Hayworth, how personal it was with him and how badly they wanted to win that ballgame…I felt like they played better than I anticipated they would. They were just a better physical team than I thought they were gonna be that night, so we felt real fortunate that we were able to win the game."

Wylie had eliminated Granbury two years in a row in the first round of the playoffs. Wylie's senior quarterback, Ronnie Cross, had stayed cool under pressure and played his trump card—Doug Gollahon—when the Pirates needed a big play in the game's closing moments.

"For whatever reason, I don't think Granbury ever adjusted to our veer pass," Doug remembered. "We used it quite a bit during the night, and I guess they just didn't expect us to go back to it. There's nothing really special about that play. It's just a straight pass, and we used it all season long."

By maintaining his composure under pressure, Ronnie personified Coach Shaffer's coaching style. Coach Shaffer preferred that his players remained calm and collected before and during games as opposed to being fired up, which is the attitude that a majority of people associate with the game of football.

"It's a little different throwing a touchdown on a play driving it in with time running out in the game, not just in the quarter," Coach Shaffer stated. "To have the poise, the composure to get it done at that point rather than in the first quarter…it's a whole different set of circumstances and emotions. Doing that elevated Ronnie's confidence quite a bit, and also elevated him in the esteem of his teammates. And of course, it didn't hurt his standing with me that he performed so well under adverse circumstances. You look for that in a person of leadership. It just makes a difference in the circumstances under which they're performing."

"Ronnie showed everybody what he was capable of doing," Roy Fuentes said. "We all believed in Ronnie, but I think Ronnie believed more in Ronnie after that game. I think he knew he could do it, but knowing that he had the confidence of all of us guys made a big difference."

Engineering that winning drive solidified Ronnie Cross's position as the starting quarterback for the Pirates the rest of the way. Ronnie's presence at quarterback turned out to be huge for Wylie's remaining four games, especially against Breckenridge for the regional championship the week after Granbury.

West Rusk helped the Pirates out in the bi-district round of the playoffs by upsetting Kaufman, 7-6. Somehow, West Rusk had managed to contain Peely Jones, and as a result, the team that beat Wylie, 53-33, in week two would not be an obstacle in the Pirates' march through the playoffs (following the win over Kaufman, West Rusk lost to Mount Vernon, 20-7, in the regional championship).

"I was so glad (Kaufman) got upset in bi-district play," Coach Shaffer said. "It would have been horrible to try to play them again, because they were really, really physically talented—so much better than we were, speed-wise, and all that stuff."

Following the win over Granbury, the Pirates were on to the regional playoffs, equaling the deepest penetration to date for a Wylie football team. They had reached the regional playoffs in twice in the last six years only to lose by a lopsided margin both times. Now, in 1977, the regional opponent was the Breckenridge Buckaroos, who upset Jacksboro, 24-12, in the bi-district playoffs before meeting Wylie. Could the Pirates get over the regional hump?

"As a coach, what we had taught the players about was that once you're out of the district and you're playing on a given night in the playoffs, anything can happen and any team can line up and beat another team on that one night," Bruce King said. "Even though you talk about that a lot, you try to get that sense of urgency into every play, every snap and down. That circumstance builds, and it kind of makes believers out of everybody at that point."

The Breckenridge game the following week proved Coach King's words to be true—anything can happen on a Friday night in the playoffs.

Regional Playoff, Wylie vs. Breckenridge

The Pirates took the field at Kangaroo Stadium in Weatherford again the night of November 25 as clear underdogs to a much faster and much larger Breckenridge team with a storied tradition.

Breckenridge was a small town situated about an hour's drive east of Abilene in Central Texas and about an hour's drive west of Weatherford, where the playoff game was to be played. In fact, some of the Breckenridge players had not even heard of the Wylie High School located in Wylie, Texas.

"There was Abilene Wylie (High School), and that's the only Wylie I'd ever heard of before we played Wylie," said Breckenridge running back/middle linebacker/place-kicker Mike Funderburg, who was a sophomore in the fall of 1977. His older brother, Johnny Funderburg, was a senior who played offensive guard and linebacker for the Buckaroos.

Actually, to say that Wylie was an underdog for this one was an understatement. To epitomize the Pirates' plight against Breckenridge, one needed only to see the mismatch of Wylie's offensive line compared to the Buckaroos' defensive front players. The Breckenridge nose guard that lined up against center Bob Skipwith was between 230 and 240 pounds, by Bob's estimation; Bob weighed a cool 165.

"I remember walking out (before the game) and us looking, going, 'Oh my gosh, these guys are monsters!'" Tony Garner said of his first impression of Breckenridge. "All the talk we heard was nothing but how big the front line was, and how fast they were…I'm sure there was some major anxiety of, 'is this gonna be a repeat (of the 1976 regional playoff against Bowie)?'"

"They were huge from both the size standpoint and the numbers standpoint," Rickey Blackman said of Breckenridge. "We had about 30 kids, and I can remember lining up for the pregame warm-ups, and they had every kid from the varsity and JV. There must have been 100 kids out there. That was just intimidating. But we knew we had a game, and the coaches obviously had us well-prepared."

Coach Bruce King said of the Breckenridge Buckaroos, "Breckenridge was certainly a really physical team, capable of just lining up and running over us at times. That was the biggest mismatch we faced during the course of the year, other than Bellville (in the state championship)."

Most everyone knew that if the Pirates were going to advance beyond the regional playoff game for the first time in their history, it would take an upset of Buster Douglas-Mike Tyson proportions.

The Breckenridge players liked those odds.

"I do remember we were very confident going into the game," Mike Funderburg stated. "We were younger that year. We had about four or five sophomores starting, so we had a younger team than Wylie."

The Breckenridge Buckaroos had achieved their lofty status in 1977 by running the Houston splitback veer offense with several punishing running backs, hence they rarely needed to pass the ball.

"Breckenridge was averaging right at 50 points a game," Coach Shaffer recalled. "One of the highest scoring high school football teams in history. They scored more than 500 points going into the regional game. They were a remarkably skilled and able and physically good football team…it was just a foregone conclusion that we didn't have a chance."

The Pirates weren't going to just hand it over, however. As was the custom throughout the playoffs, the outlook of the Pirate players was different from that of many so-called "football experts" who predicted the odds. Roy Fuentes summed up the team's feelings before that game: "From the coaches' perspective, if we could keep it close…that was our whole goal, to keep it close, and you never know what might happen. One mistake, one turnover can turn around the game."

Knowing that Breckenridge was heavily favored to win the playoff game, Coach Shaffer searched for a way to inspire his team in the days before the playoff game. What resulted was a tradition that remains a large part of Wylie High School athletics and of the Wylie community to this day—AHMO.

When Coach Shaffer returned home from a late practice on the Monday following the Granbury game, he turned on his television to watch *Dean Martin's Celebrity Roast*, a popular comedy show where several celebrities would gather to playfully "roast," or insult another celebrity. On this particular episode, the celebrity being roasted was Dan Haggerty, best known at the time for playing James "Grizzly" Adams on the television series, *The Life and Times of Grizzly Adams*. The program was about a fugitive mountain man who befriended a large grizzly bear.

One of the comedians roasting Haggerty on the Dean Martin program spoke of his upbringing on the South Side of Chicago. This comedian was talking about the street language he had used in his youth, and one of the words he said was "AHMO" as in "AHMO kick your butt."

This gave Coach Shaffer an idea. The next day, he told his team about the new word he had picked up on television, and when the Pirates huddled in practice, they shouted "AHMO" as they broke from the huddle. They continued shouting their new word throughout the rest of the week in practice.

The whole thing snowballed from there. AHMO soon became synonymous with Pirate football, much the same way "Mojo" (taken from a Wilson Pickett song) had become with Odessa Permian High School in West Texas. AHMO was shoe polished on cars and seen on signs throughout the town of Wylie throughout the rest of the 1977 playoffs after the Breckenridge game.

Coach Shaffer recalled that he told his team, "There's a bunch of guys in Breckenridge who are figuring you aren't going to be much. But I want you to remind yourself when you go to the line of scrimmage, 'AHMO kick your butt.'"

Armed with a new battle cry, if you will, the Pirates felt ready to take on the world. Against the Breckenridge Buckaroos—who were in the playoffs for the first time in 16 years—Wylie soon came crashing to earth.

On Breckenridge's first offensive series, Wylie lost defensive tackle Tim Pelton to a broken leg. But he did not go quietly—as was typical of the Wylie Pirates, Tim wanted to play no matter how much it hurt, and he protested being relegated to the bench.

"We had to kind of force him out, because he couldn't stand up on it," Wayne Mayberry said.

"(Tim) wanted to get back in the game so bad, I can remember him jogging or trying to exercise on the sideline," Rickey Blackman recalled. "I don't remember how bad it was broken, but I know that Tim is a pretty tough guy and he was still trying to fight through the pain and still trying to keep on playing. They finally figured out it was broken...I remember he was still over there trying to get back in the game somehow, and I've always remembered that."

In came sophomore Mike "Klink" Helm, who had played in place of defensive tackle Chuck Edge a week earlier against Granbury. Ironically, Mike's parents had asked Coach Page early in the 1977 season if Mike would be better off playing for the junior varsity team, since as a sophomore he was not getting much playing time with the varsity team.

"I said 'No, I need him. He's one injury away from doing it,'" Coach Page remembered. And lo and behold, it happened. Though the Pirates missed Tim's toughness in the lineup the rest of the way, Mike's play at defensive tackle in the playoffs was stellar.

"Mike was a sophomore, and kind of an unknown player at the time," Rickey Blackman said. "He came in and played great, and I think that's another tribute to the coaching staff. It seemed like everybody that came in and stepped in for somebody else did really well. Tim was a really good player, but Mike came in and played pretty well as well."

About halfway through the first quarter, the Buckaroos' Wade Stanford crossed the goal line from a yard out for the first score. Stanford had set up the touchdown with a 38-yard run, and Mike Funderburg's extra point put Breckenridge up, 7-0.

The Wylie offense, meanwhile, was squandering its chances, partly because of the Buckaroos defense and partly because of a failure to execute. The larger Breckenridge defenders were difficult to block, namely one Artis Cavanaugh. The Pirates who had the monumental task of blocking Artis were Phil Lemons, who at left offensive tackle lined up directly across from him, and Chuck Edge at left guard.

"Coach Page told me at the first of the week that a lot of it was dependent on how well I took care of my man," Phil explained. "I was very, very nervous about it. We had a couple of plays where we'd go on a no snap count, and I remember trying to get a jump on him. I knew I was not supposed to go until the ball was snapped, and started leaning and fell flat on my butt. I knew I wasn't supposed to move. I was trying not to move, and I got pretty well chewed on at halftime for not concentrating enough."

Sometimes in that game, the Wylie offensive line got the job done and sometimes they did not. In all, the Buckaroos' defenders sacked Ronnie Cross seven times on the evening. But he also completed 16 passes, including several on the game-winning drive in the game's final minute.

"Offensively, I'd have to say Artis Cavanaugh from Breckenridge was the toughest guy that I've ever had to play against," Chuck said. "He was 6-foot-6, 240-ish. I couldn't block him."

Following Breckenridge's touchdown in the first quarter, the Buckaroos gifted Wylie good field position at midfield with a personal foul. The Pirates drove to the seven, and on fourth down, Coach Shaffer reached into his bag of tricks.

The Pirates tried a fake field goal, but Ronnie's pass intended for Mark Whitehead in the end zone fell incomplete and they turned it over on downs. Wylie's next possession ended abruptly deep in Breckenridge territory when the Buckaroos recovered a fumble by Wendell Collins, who finished as the Pirates' leading rusher in the game with 40 yards on seven attempts.

The Buckaroos eventually fumbled on that drive and Rickey Blackman recovered at the Breckenridge 18. But Wylie again turned it over on downs when the Buckaroos' Rocky Cozart broke up Ronnie's pass, intended for Tony Garner, on fourth down. The ensuing Breckenridge drive led to a 25-yard field goal by Mike Funderburg to increase the Buckaroos' lead to 10-0 with four minutes left in the first half. The score stayed at 10-0 until the intermission.

The Pirate defense had done its part in the first 24 minutes of the game, but the offense had done little in the first half except waste a few golden opportunities. Limiting Breckenridge to 10 first-half points can be attributed to a change in the defensive scheme.

In every game of the 1977 season prior to this one, the Pirates had run a basic 4-3 or 6-1 defense, one in which the defensive ends would line up against the offensive tackles, the defensive tackles would line up against the offensive guards and the outside linebackers would line up at the line of scrimmage. The coaches decided that Breckenridge was such a physically superior team that the defensive schemes they had used all season long would not work.

"When we played Breckenridge, we changed that up and left the ends out over the tight ends and moved the linebackers up out over the tackles," Coach Page said. "We did a lot of looping and slanting and just really mixed up the front there and presented them with something they'd never seen before. I think the confusion they had in their blocking schemes led to us being able to play with them."

Of the mismatch on the offensive line, Bob Skipwith remarked, "I felt like I could get into (the nose guard's) feet. Oftentimes, I was down crawling on people's feet and legs, just tying 'em up, because I couldn't physically stand there and line up and go head-to-head with 'em. I had to use some advantage. I'd take their feet out from under 'em a time or two, and then when they'd get down low to prevent me from doing that, then I'd come up and catch 'em off guard in that fashion."

On the size mismatch as well as the numbers mismatch, Rickey Blackman stated, "They had big kids to begin with, and then on top of that, just the sheer number of 'em. I think it's a credit to the team that we hung in there with the players we had versus the style and the amount of players that they had."

Roy Fuentes recalled that this was an extremely physical Breckenridge team. In fact, for him the Breckenridge game supplanted the regional playoff against Bowie in 1976 as the most physical game in which he had played.

"They had thrown their best at us," Roy recalled, "and we were losing, but we were hanging tough with them. I think not getting blown out in that first half gave us a lot of confidence."

Chuck Edge stated, "Coach Shaffer told us many years later that he was just tickled to death going into halftime down 10-0. He thought to himself, 'If we play this well again next half, it'll only be 20-0.'"

But the players did not share this sentiment at the time. As it turned out, the mood in the Pirates' locker room was quite different than what Coach Shaffer expected going in. They were anything but tickled. Most, if not all, of the Wylie players were upset that they were not closer to Breckenridge than 10 points. Some Pirates, if not all, felt they should have been ahead at the intermission.

"As they came off the field (for halftime), it was a 10-0 ballgame, and our kids were mad," Coach Shaffer said. "They were visibly angry with themselves for not having played better…it was clear that they really believed that they could beat that bunch."

As a result of the Pirates' anger over not having executed on offense, Coach Shaffer told his staff he was going to approach the second half differently than he did the first—he was now going to coach with the attitude that Wylie should be winning instead of Wylie being the massive underdog. And in an effort to "confirm" what he overheard that the kids believed they could beat Breckenridge, in Coach Shaffer's own words, "I went in and I chewed butt. I got after them a little bit. Not super hard, but I let them know that I agreed with them."

Offensive tackle Phil Lemons is one that took Coach Shaffer's counsel to heart, since he had missed a blocking assignment on Artis Cavanaugh in the first half. "He said that we weren't concentrating enough and that we lacked concentration, and if we were going to win, we were going to have to concentrate more," Phil said.

"We had reached a point together as a team where we felt like we could play with anybody," Rock King said. "We knew what we could do as far as execution and how we should do things. That was a big thing, the disappointment in the fact that we just didn't do what we felt like we should have done. We made some mistakes. We didn't make good adjustments. We didn't make good reads. And so we felt like they were beating us, not because they were that much better than us, but because we were not playing up to our potential. It would have been different if we'd been doing everything right and they were up 10-0."

Strong safety Tony Garner recalled a brief halftime conversation with Coach Bruce King, the Pirates' secondary coach. According to Tony, Coach King told him, "It's in you guys' hands. There's nothing we have that we can do or say that's gonna change it. You're either gonna come out and play football or you're not."

"We had so many missed opportunities in the first half," Ronnie Cross remembered. "We actually probably should have been ahead at halftime. We missed scoring opportunities a couple of times and had a lot of passes dropped. We just made a lot of mistakes. We were pretty hot about it as a team, if I remember the locker room conversations well. We were pretty chapped that we weren't in the lead, and that's probably the best thing that ever happened to us, because we came out in the second half and just totally shut Breckenridge down."

Eventually, that is what happened. But Coach Shaffer's halftime pep talk did not take immediate effect as far as the offense was concerned. Neither team dented the scoreboard in the third quarter, and time was running out on the Wylie Pirates. Early in the fourth quarter, the Pirates recovered a muffed punt at the Breckenridge 30 yard line.

The Pirates were again gifted the short field, but could not do anything with it. The drive ended when Mike Funderburg, Breckenridge's talented sophomore middle linebacker, sacked Ronnie Cross on fourth down.

The Buckaroos immediately gave the ball to Wade Stanford, who ripped off a large gain to the Wylie 19. It appeared that Breckenridge was on its way to putting the game out of reach. But with time ticking away, the Wylie defense clamped down and forced Breckenridge to turn it over on downs, and the Pirates began their large uphill climb at their own 18.

Ronnie led the Pirates down the field, helped out by a 42-yard pass play to Roy Fuentes up the sideline. Roy was tackled from behind at the Breckenridge 28. The Buckaroos responded by sacking Ronnie for a 10-yard loss, but Wendell Collins took the ball and ran it 21 yards for the first down. Wylie finally cracked the scoreboard with a 17-yard touchdown pass from Ronnie to Roy McClendon with just over three minutes remaining.

With the score 10-6, Coach Shaffer opted to have the Pirates go for a two-point conversion rather than kick the extra point and make it 10-7. By going for two, Coach Shaffer wanted to avoid a 10-10 tie should the Pirates drive down later and kick a field goal; a tie would have given Breckenridge the win based on having the most offensive penetrations (the UIL did not adopt overtime in Texas high school football until 1995).

But Ronnie's pass on the two-point attempt fell incomplete, leaving the score at 10-6 and leaving the Pirates in need of another touchdown.

The Pirates attempted an onside kick, but the Buckaroos received possession when the ball did not go the required 10 yards. The play turned out to be costly for Breckenridge, however. The struggle to recover the ball on the onside kick resulted in a scuffle, which in turn resulted in the ejection of Mike Funderburg. Breckenridge would have to finish the game without one of its best defensive players.

Not only did the Buckaroos lose Mike Funderburg, but they were penalized 15 yards for a personal foul on the play, thus causing them to lose field position. The penalty pushed the Buckaroos back to their own 31, rather than near midfield at the 46 where the onside kick was recovered.

Still, Breckenridge was mostly a running team, and they could seal the game with only one first down. But the Wylie defense toughened, and the Buckaroos went three and out, failing to get that one first down that would have clinched it for them. In fact, they gained only one yard on the three plays combined. The Pirates got the ball back on their own 24 with 1:42 remaining after a punt.

What ensued did not seem promising for Wylie. Mike Funderburg was gone, but the Buckaroos still had Artis Cavanaugh, and big Artis made his presence felt when he sacked Ronnie Cross for an eight-yard loss to the 16 on the drive's first play. Now the end zone was 84 yards away with just over a minute remaining. Two incomplete passes later, the Pirates stared at a third and 18 situation.

Ronnie and Doug Gollahon hooked up for only a five-yard gain, and the Pirates would have faced fourth and 13 had not an overzealous Buckaroos defender hit Doug after the whistle blew. The 15-yard late hit penalty gave the Pirates a first down at their own 36. Wylie had new life.

But the suspense was not over. Two incomplete passes later, on third and 10, Ronnie completed a pass to Roy Fuentes for six yards, putting the Pirates in a fourth and four situation.

In the crunch, Ronnie looked to his tight end, Doug Gollahon, with the old "flea flicker" play, similar to the hook and ladder. Ronnie threw a high, hard one to his tight end, who outleaped several green jerseys to come down with the football. Doug then lateraled to Wendell Collins, the pitch back who was trailing the play, and Wendell gained the necessary yardage for the first down at midfield with 39 seconds left.

In the third game of the season, against Farmersville, the Pirates scored a touchdown using that same flea flicker play with Rock King at quarterback, Garth Touchstone at tight end and Wayne Mayberry at running back. The Pirates were able to execute when the play was called no matter who the personnel were.

"It's a short curl route," Doug said of the flea flicker play. "The running back, which was Wendell Collins, comes out of the backfield toward the sideline. They threw me the ball, and I just pitched it to Wendell coming out the backfield and he's on a full sprint coming toward the sideline. I'm on his inside and he runs to my outside, between me and the sideline. I had to catch the ball and pitch it back to him. It's all a timing deal…I remember the pass was a little bit high and I had to jump up to get it. When I caught the ball, I saw Wendell there and I didn't have time to come back to the ground, or he'd have been by me and it would have been a forward lateral. While I was in the air, I just threw it like a basketball pass."

According to Ronnie Cross, the flea flicker was the play the Pirates intended to run a few plays earlier when Doug drew the personal foul penalty, but the timing of the play was not conducive to pitching the ball. It worked on the second try, and the Pirates were in business.

After a four-yard pass completion to Wendell Collins and a 16-yarder on an out route to Tony Garner moved the ball to the Breckenridge 30, where the Pirates called a timeout with one second left.

According to Phil Lemons, who operated a clock at basketball games in Dimmit, Texas, for many years, it took a little luck for the Pirates to get that one second. "Just a split second, a flick of the switch, and that game could have been overwith. Not intentional, but any hesitation at all (by the clockkeeper), and that game would have been overwith."

But as it was, the Pirates had their one second. This was it. There was time for one more play. This play had to result in a 30-yard touchdown or Wylie's season was over and Breckenridge would advance to the next round.

"We joined hands and said, 'We've come too far to quit now,' in the huddle before that last play," Jess Croley recalled. "That's the first time we decided we weren't gonna get beat."

The AHMO was starting to flow. Ronnie Cross had led the Pirates downfield for a last-minute game-winning drive the week before against Granbury on that very same field in Weatherford. He understood pressure. Could he do it again?

"You take Ronnie Cross and you line him up and tell him after a time out…he knows, when there's a time out made, with one second left to go in that game, he knows it's going to be a pass," Coach Shaffer explained. "And he knows this is going to be a touchdown or the last time he'll ever throw a football in his high school career."

Nothing in the Pirates' playbook would do for this pressure situation. This is where being well-coached came in real handy.

Coach King and Coach Page were forced to vacate their seats in the press box because they could not hear well enough to communicate with Coach Shaffer over the phones, largely because of the deafening crowd noise. They had walked down the bleachers and to the Wylie sideline just before Tony Garner caught the pass that brought the ball to the 30.

Coach King did not typically call plays; Coach Shaffer was the one largely responsible for the Pirates' play calling. Coach King's duties during the game included feeding Coach Shaffer information about what the opposing secondary and linebackers were doing regarding the pass (Coach Page fed information about the opposing front seven and the linebackers regarding the run). But for this situation, Coach King had an idea.

Nothing got by the Wylie coaches. Coach King noticed that Breckenridge had removed a linebacker and placed an extra man in the secondary to play safety; but he also noticed that even though it was a type of zone coverage, the cornerbacks were getting close to the outside receivers and almost playing a man-to-man type defense.

With this information, Coach King suggested that they use a play they had not used since the last offensive play of the 1976 regional playoff game against Bowie. The circumstances were much different then—the Pirates were on the short end of a rout against Bowie. This time, the coaches figured they would try a similar play in which everyone on the right side blocks up and the flanker goes out for a pass as a decoy, running a hard post route and faking the cornerback into the middle of the field, according to Coach King. The pass would go to the tight end lined up on the left side, who would run a flag route.

"It isolates that one outside deep defender," Coach Shaffer said, "and for a long time, he's on his man and he is afraid to get beat deep. The (flanker) comes down there and gets his attention and moves him to the inside slightly, and because of the pressure of the circumstance, his focus narrows, he doesn't see the (tight end) coming underneath to the outside, and (the tight end) is momentarily open."

In the blowout playoff loss to Bowie the year before, this play resulted in a touchdown for Wylie. During crunch time against Breckenridge, Bruce King remembered this and suggested to Coach Shaffer that they use a similar play.

The Pirates had yet to run the play in 1977. In fact, they had not even practiced it. Since that was the case, Coach King had to literally draw the play in the dirt on the sideline so the Pirate players could visualize where they were supposed to go on the play. The pass was to go to Roy Fuentes, who normally played flanker on offense but for this play lined up as the tight end on the strong side while Tony Garner lined up at flanker as the decoy.

"The sidelines were worn down," Coach King recalled. "It was just dirt there, so we just kind of knelt down and said, 'This is exactly what we want to do, and Roy, if you'll run down kind of make your break in behind where Tony's gonna run to the middle of the field, then Ronnie will try to throw the ball to the corner over there,' and that's kind of the way that went."

The AHMO was really working by this time, and the play turned out to be just what the doctor ordered.

Bob Skipwith snapped the ball to Ronnie and the play was on. With the Buckaroos running a prevent defense, knowing the Pirates would pass the ball—and expecting them to throw into the end zone—they concentrated more on stopping the pass than on rushing the passer. Hence, Ronnie had all the time he needed to throw. Chuck Edge remembered that he and Phil Lemons were able to block Artis Cavanaugh on that play with the help of the blocking tight end, Doug Gollahon. "He still almost got there (to the quarterback)," Chuck said. "But we held him off long enough."

Tony ran his post route to the middle and Roy ran the flag route up the left sideline and got open; Ronnie's pass was a tad underthrown and Roy had to wait on it, but he hauled it in at the two and maneuvered his way across the goal line for the game-winning touchdown with no time left on the clock. He was actually hit from behind on the play by a Breckenridge defender.

"The defenders were definitely back in the end zone, trying to prevent us from getting into the end zone," Roy remembered. "Being designed to stop short of the goal line, that caught them off guard. Luckily, it was a good pass by Ronnie, and I was able to catch it and get into the end zone.

"It was slightly underthrown," Roy continued, "but it actually worked out for the better, I think. If he'd overthrown it at all, the defender would have had a better chance at coming up and knocking it down or hitting it away."

According to Bruce King, the use of Tony Garner at flanker as a decoy worked like a charm. "(The flanker) just jumped on (the cornerback) and ran him right into the middle of the field, which was running right into that other safety, so it held the safety in the middle of the field. The cornerback who should have picked up the outside third there for a zone-type coverage, he was locked onto that flanker not wanting him to catch a ball. So Roy lined up at tight end and ran a flag-type pattern, and he broke to the wide open field. There was nobody in there. I think that was just divine intervention, how all that came together."

Many believe it was the AHMO.

Wylie fans charged onto the field and the Pirates celebrated with a massive dogpile as the shocked Breckenridge players and fans looked on in disbelief. The chaos on the field prevented the Pirates from attempting the extra point, but it did not matter. The Pirates were 12-10 victors and had held the Buckaroos scoreless in the second half. The Breckenridge faithful hoped and waited desperately for a flag that would nullify the touchdown by Roy Fuentes, but it never came. The crowd noise, which had reached epic proportions coming from both sides before that final play, was now coming from only one side of the bleachers—Wylie's. The Breckenridge fans were silent.

"People were just nuts," Ronnie Cross recalled of the post-game celebration. "The fences around the football field were bent over from people rushing the field. Nobody on either side of that stadium was sitting down in the last three or four minutes of that ballgame. Nobody that was at that game, whether it was on the field, or in the stands, or in the press box, will ever forget that game…it was just fun to be a part of that. That was the coolest thing, the way we just never gave up."

As for Breckenridge, mistakes—especially those on the Pirates' game-winning drive—had cost the team dearly. Both teams had made mistakes, but when it came down to it, Wylie had made fewer.

"There's a lot of ifs, ands or buts, but basically, they were more disciplined than we were," Mike Funderburg remembered. "I just remember it being a tough ballgame all the way down to the end. We thought we had the game won, and our dang defensive back fell down (on the last touchdown), and that's all she wrote."

On the way to the dressing room several minutes after the game-winning play, Ronnie Cross and Roy Fuentes had to stop and just soak it all in.

"We could barely breathe at the bottom of that pile," Roy stated. "By the time we got up, we were so exhausted. Physically, we were exhausted—we got beat up the entire game. Mentally, we were exhausted. I don't think I've ever had that feeling of just total exhaustion again. It was so neat to be involved in that play."

Wylie had won, and a personal foul penalty figured prominently in the game-winning drive for the Pirates just as it had a week earlier against Granbury. And one of the big reasons the Pirates were able to beat Breckenridge, according to Rock King, was Wylie's ability to make adjustments to handle Breckenridge's virtual physical domination at the line of scrimmage, which the Pirates had expected from studying the game films.

"We had guys that were smart up on the offensive line that knew how to call blocking schemes and make adjustments," Rock explained. "Ronnie did a good job of making audibles at the line of scrimmage, reading defenses…we were always doing that."

The game was fairly even as far as statistics go—15 first downs for Wylie, 14 for Breckenridge. Wylie had 236 total yards while Breckenridge had 233. Most of the Buckaroos' yardage came on the ground (221), led by 124 yards for Wade Stanford on 17 carries. The Buckaroos attempted only four passes and completed just one for 12 yards.

Wylie, meanwhile, gained 97 yards rushing and 139 passing (Ronnie completed 16 of 35 with one interception). Doug Gollahon led the Pirates with seven receptions.

But no matter how well the statistics for the two teams matched, the Wylie Pirates were ahead in the only column that mattered when the final whistle blew.

The Pirates were regional champions for the first time in their history. From there, it was to the state quarterfinals, where no Wylie team had gone before.

In Wylie, the play that beat Breckenridge in 1977 is still talked about. The Pittsburgh Steelers of the NFL had their "Immaculate Reception," which occurred on the last play of a 1972 playoff game against the Oakland Raiders—a play on which Franco Harris made shoestring catch of a deflected pass to score a 60-yard Pittsburgh touchdown on the last play of the game. The Dallas Cowboys had theirs, a "Hail Mary" bomb from Roger Staubach to Drew Pearson in the final minute to beat the Minnesota Vikings in the 1975 playoffs.

After the playoff game with Breckenridge, the Wylie Pirates had their own version of the "Immaculate Reception."

One ironic side note about Wylie's "Immaculate Reception" is that Coach Shaffer was reportedly not fond of his receivers running flag routes. "He felt like it was real difficult to execute and make that catch, because they were catching over their shoulder," Bruce King explained. " Plus, they didn't have real good vision on the ball all the time. So we didn't run that kind of a route very often. He didn't want us calling plays or saying, 'Let's run this play, or let's run this play.' But he said, 'If you see something, or if you want to run a play, we'll run your play. But you need to be sure.' In that situation, that was just one of those deals that with one second left, and under those circumstances, I don't think anybody would have argued about, 'Well, what can we do?'"

Coach King was sure, and the rest was history.

The play brought joy to the people Wylie, but broke many a heart in Breckenridge. "When you experience something like that, you feel something like that, it just kills you," Mike Funderburg described. "That was hard, hard for me to take. I remember it crushed Johnny, my brother. I mean, it just crushed him. He probably took it harder than I did, because I was a sophomore."

Mike said to this day he still thinks about seeing the late hit on Doug Gollahon that gave the Pirates a first down on the winning drive, and also seeing the Pirates scoring the winning touchdown. "It never goes away," Mike said.

But even though his team lost in such a heartbreaking fashion, Mike was quick to add, "That's the best you can get in high school football, that kind of game."

Ronnie Cross had pulled it off for the Pirate two weeks in a row in two of the highest pressure situations that any quarterback could have faced.

"During the championship run in the playoffs, Ronnie really made the plays when he had to," Rickey Blackman recalled. "The Breckenridge score…it was pretty amazing to do that."

After two miracle wins in the playoffs, the Wylie Pirates' confidence had increased immeasurably. As the cliché goes, the Pirates were confident, but not cocky, headed into the state quarterfinal against Mount Vernon.

"If we'd beaten (Breckenridge) 30-17 in a conventional fashion, we probably wouldn't have won the state championship," Coach Shaffer recalled. "Because it wouldn't have built the kind of confidence that that sort of thing does."

Tony Garner said of the attitude following the Breckenridge game, which made Wylie one of the final eight teams left in Class 2A, "I think once we did win that one-second game, it was kind of like, 'Hey, there's only eight of us left at this point. We've got an opportunity (to go all the way).'"

"I don't think any of us thought about losing again," Chuck Edge explained of the Pirates' mentality after beating Breckenridge. "It was like catching a second wind."

Coach Bruce King stated of the importance of Wylie's win over Breckenridge, "It just lifted us to a completely different level of confidence and understanding, and all the kids became immersed in the thing. With five or six of the guys, it was like having coaches on the field. Everybody understood the relevance of what can happen on any one snap of the ball, and it just elevated our game to a completely different level."

Mike Funderburg correctly assessed the situation of the winner of the Wylie-Breckenridge game before the game even took place, having no idea just how right he would be. "I knew that whoever won that game would probably win state, and that's the way it turned out. We knew that if we'd beaten Wylie…they were the best team left in the playoffs, and whoever won that game would probably win (state). Sure enough, it turned out that way."

And AHMO was a permanent part of football in Wylie, Texas.

State Quarterfinal Playoff, Wylie vs. Mount Vernon

For the quarterfinal game, the Wylie Pirates once again needed to overcome a faster, larger opponent in the form of the Mount Vernon Tigers, which some 22 years earlier featured a standout quarterback named Don Meredith (later of Southern Methodist University, Dallas Cowboys and Monday Night Football fame). But the Pirates had handled bigger, stronger and faster opponents before—more than once.

To get to the quarterfinal playoff, Mount Vernon had posted wins over Linden-Kildare in bi-district (27-14) and over West Rusk in the regional playoffs (20-7). This was the same West Rusk team that knocked out Kaufman in bi-district play that year.

The Pirates always had the staunch support of the people of Wylie, and it was mounting with each playoff game. Kenneth Nall, who operated a clothing factory in Downtown Wylie in 1977 and employed several mothers of kids who played on the football team, recalled that after the games were over a caravan would head to someone's house in town and everyone would talk about the game until the wee hours of the morning. Then, the following week, they would continue to talk about the game. "We were wrapped up in it," Kenneth remembered.

A few days before the state quarterfinal, Wylie Mayor William E. Martin declared that the Wylie Pirates now officially had the town's support. Mayor Martin issued a proclamation on November 28 declaring that week as "Wylie Pirates Week." In that proclamation, Mayor Martin encouraged the whole town to attend the quarterfinal game against Mount Vernon and "support and cheer your team to victory."

By Coach Shaffer's recollection, on the night of the Wylie-Breckenridge game, some Mount Vernon scouts who attended that game went to a restaurant afterward and happened upon some Wylie scouts who had attended the Mount Vernon-West Rusk game. The Mount Vernon scouts said they had left that Wylie-Breckenridge contest early, thinking Breckenridge had the game in hand and that their team would be playing Breckenridge. They had underestimated the power of AHMO.

The two scouting staffs exchanged the scores from the regional playoff games from that night, and Mount Vernon learned they would be playing Wylie and not Breckenridge as they had planned.

"I'm sure they found that to be a great relief," Coach Shaffer said with a laugh. "They were probably thinking, 'Boy, I'm sure glad that Breckenridge didn't win, because we could have never played with Breckenridge…this Wylie team, they were just lucky as a skunk to have won.'"

By the time Wylie was finished with Mount Vernon in the state quarterfinal on the night of December 2 at the brand new Mesquite Memorial Stadium, the Tigers would probably have rather taken their chances with Breckenridge. Ronnie Cross, who started and played the majority of the game at quarterback for the Pirates, said simply of Mount Vernon, "We just ate them up."

The Tigers did everything they could to try to stop the Wylie passing game, but it was no use. Ronnie posted his best passing game of the year, completing 11 of 19 passes for 224 yards. What made that all the more amazing was that by his own recollection, Ronnie called "70 percent" of that game at the line of scrimmage by checking off the Mount Vernon defense.

"They had all these different defenses, and I knew what defenses we could run certain plays against and what defenses we couldn't," Ronnie said. "We'd call a play in the huddle and go up to the line of scrimmage, and they'd be set in a defense that we couldn't run the play that we called in the huddle."

After receiving the opening kickoff, the Pirates began a lengthy scoring drive, helped out by two big plays—one a pass interference call on the Tigers and one a 45-yard completion from Ronnie to Doug Gollahon that set them up on the Tiger 19. On the next play, Wayne Mayberry followed the block of Wendell Collins around the left side and bulled in for the touchdown. After Rock King's extra point, it was 7-0, Pirates, just two minutes into the game.

Mount Vernon made a big push to establish the running game early, and that is exactly what they did. The Tigers picked up 124 yards rushing in the first half. On their next possession following the Wylie touchdown, David Cates nailed a 34-yard field goal with five minutes left in the first quarter for Mount Vernon's first points.

In the second quarter, the Pirates gifted the Tigers great field position with a fumble on the Wylie 17. It took seven plays, but eventually Brad Lowry punched it in from a yard out and David Cates kicked the PAT to put Wylie in a 10-7 hole. Just as they had in the first two playoff games, the Pirates found themselves on the short end of the score early.

But having been in that situation before and overcome it more than once, the Pirates knew they could do it again.

And once they got started on the comeback trail, it did not take long. After Dale Morgan returned the ensuing kickoff to midfield, the Wylie offense began its quest.

Ten plays later, Wayne Mayberry scored from two yards out. The Tigers sacked Ronnie on the two-point conversion attempt, but Wylie had the lead at 13-10. On Mount Vernon's next possession, they made a curious decision to go for it on fourth and five from their own 31. Perhaps more than anything, going for it deep in their own territory in the second quarter down by only three points spoke volumes about how few chances the Tigers thought they were going to get against the Wylie defense.

It was not to be for Mount Vernon on this fourth down play. Bruce "Doc" Cryer, now the Pirates' starting middle linebacker, stuffed the Tigers for no gain and the ball went over to Wylie on downs.

It took the Pirates just two plays to capitalize on the gift. One play was a 15-yard completion from Ronnie Cross to Tony Garner, and the other was a 16-yard run by Ronnie for the touchdown. Rock missed the extra point, but the Pirates had a nine-point lead at 19-10 and had some breathing room.

The Tigers tried to run the ball in the second half just as they did in the first, but were repeatedly foiled by the Wylie defense. Much of the ineffectiveness of the Tiger running game can be attributed to the work of Wylie's coaching staff. Mount Vernon operated out of the two-back veer similar to what Wylie ran, and when the coaches were studying the game films of Mount Vernon, they discovered that the way the Tigers' running back's feet were positioned was a tipoff as to which direction he would run.

"What Coach Shaffer had discovered in watching that film is that their full back was indicating which direction he was gonna go in that offense on every play by which foot he dropped back, either his right foot or his left foot, when he went down in his stance," said Bruce King, who coached the secondary and the receivers. "As soon as they came up to the line and got in their stance, we could make a defensive call relative to their formation, knowing exactly which way the ball was gonna go, and they only had one or two plays that they could run a counter from the way they were offensively set. So that was a big, big advantage.

"Even though they were pretty physically talented and all, that made a whole difference in the way we were able to defense them," Coach King continued.

"They were just never able to get untracked or do anything offensively against our defense."

Linebacker Rickey Blackman recalled, "The linebackers would go up every play. You can almost see us on film standing on or tiptoes trying to figure out how the running backs were lined up, and we would know exactly what the guys were gonna run. Back then, you didn't have the diverse offensive schemes that you have nowadays. We knew by the way they were lining up if they were gonna run to the right or run to the left, and we'd adjust our defense accordingly. They had some really good players, and if it had been a straight up game where we hadn't known that, it obviously would have been a lot closer. We probably would have still beaten 'em."

Utilizing Coach Shaffer's discovery from watching the films of Mount Vernon, Mark Whitehead, Jess Croley, Chuck Edge and Dale Morgan were particularly tough on the Tigers' running game. When the smoke cleared, the Tigers had gained just 53 yards rushing in the second half, less than half of their total from the first 24 minutes.

Mount Vernon did not fare much better with the pass. David Cates completed five of 12 attempts for 38 yards but the big number was three, which was the number of passes he completed to Wylie defenders named Roy (two to Fuentes and one to McClendon). Each one seemed to come at a crucial time when the Tigers were trying to rally.

"I think it all falls back to Shaffer and Page, Coach Ard and Coach King—they had done their homework," strong safety Tony Garner recalled. "When this lineman gets up there and he puts his foot back instead of up, or this receiver goes out and he has his head turned all the way in watching the ball versus straight ahead. I mean, it was a dead giveaway. They had the tendencies down so well. And they made us watch film to the point where we were just sick of film. But come game time, it wasn't a question. They'd line up, and we'd all look at each other, and there was a pass coming. It was just (a matter of) who was gonna get it."

According to Bruce King, "Offensively, we threw the ball so much, we had a lot of people that had receiving ability on both sides of the ball. People played both ways an awful lot, so they were receivers along with being players in the secondary, or even running backs that played in the secondary. They caught a lot of balls in practice, and we worked a lot offensively throwing the ball, and that translated to a big help and benefit to us on defense because people knew how to go get the ball and could catch it when they got there."

With seven minutes to play in the third quarter, the punting of Rock King came into play. Rock pinned the Tigers at their own one yard line, and on the next play, a host of Pirates dropped David Cates in the end zone for a safety and a 21-10 Pirate lead.

The Wylie offense was not finished yet. Ronnie Cross connected with Doug Gollahon for a 56-yard touchdown bomb on the Pirates' next drive. After a Roy Fuentes interception gave the Pirates the ball back, Ronnie dropped another bomb on Mount Vernon with a 39-yard scoring pass to Garth Touchstone with just under four minutes remaining in the third. It was Wylie's final score of the game, but by then, it was well in hand.

"We had a great night all the way around," Ronnie Cross said. "The defense played well. The offense was on a roll. After Breckenridge, I think we could have played the (Dallas) Cowboys. Realistically, we couldn't have, but it was kind of one of those feelings where we thought we could beat anybody after we did what we did against Breckenridge."

In the final quarter, the Tigers drove to the Pirate 30 but were again foiled on an interception by cornerback Roy Fuentes. When time ran out, the scoreboard read Wylie 35, Mount Vernon 10, with Wylie having scored 28 unanswered points.

"We knew enough to where we could set our defense to give us a distinct advantage," Coach Shaffer explained. "and we just shut 'em down. They had a great football team that lost in part because they tipped their hand."

"I think all throughout the year we had critical plays at critical times that made you think that something good was happening," Rickey Blackman stated. "We had a tremendous amount of confidence in the coaching staff. Coach Shaffer, obviously, was very brilliant with play-calling. Coach Page, on defense, always seemed to have us in the right place at the right time. He just made adjustments every week to react to what we anticipated the other team doing."

One play in the Mount Vernon game epitomized just how right things were going for the Pirates at that point. Early in the game, the Tigers lined up to punt on a fourth down play near midfield. The Wylie coaches remembered from the films of Mount Vernon that the Tigers liked to fake the punt by snapping the ball to the upback and having him run the ball. On this particular play, they smelled a fake and sent in Bob Skipwith, who did not usually play on punt return teams, for the sole purpose of shadowing the upback.

"They lined me up just left of their center," Bob remembered. "We worked on it in practice all week. They told me, 'Don't worry about punt coverage or the return team. Your job is to watch the upback. No matter what happens, he's your man, whether he's got the ball or not.' I lined up, and sure enough, they snapped the ball to the upback and I stopped him right in his tracks. I just hammered him.

"We never ran that punt return coverage again that game or any other time. We knew if they ran it once, they wouldn't try it again. It was sort of that one shot deal, and we stopped 'em and took the ball over right there."

Perhaps this game did not possess the suspense late in the contest that the Granbury or Breckenridge games had. But one thing was certain—the Pirates were clicking on all cylinders going into the state semifinal against Childress, and the AHMO was flowing.

State Semifinal Playoff, Wylie vs. Childress

Coach Shaffer had hoped to see this game played out close to home in a venue such as Mesquite or Plano, but the coin toss with the Childress coaches the week before to determine the time and site of the game did not go his way. The game was played on a frigid cold Saturday night—the Pirates' first Saturday game of the year—on December 10 at Wichita Falls Memorial Stadium.

The legend has it that Wylie's coaches were told by the Childress coaches when they met for the coin toss that it did not matter who would win between Wylie and Childress. The Childress coaches believed Bellville, the team ranked No. 1 in Texas by the Associated Press for much of the season, was lurking on the horizon to play the Wylie-Childress winner and was sure to win the state title.

For once in the playoffs, Wylie was not outsized. Yet once again, Wylie was considered to by the underdog by the so-called "football experts" because the Childress Bobcats had been to this point in the playoffs more than once in recent history. They had reached the state championship game in each of the previous two years only to lose to LaGrange in 1975 and Rockdale in 1976.

The 1977 Bobcats, who went into that semifinal game with a 12-1 record, were out to prove they were not "next year's champions," a moniker the Dallas Cowboys were once dubiously stuck with after losing a series of championship games (and one Super Bowl) in the late 1960s-early 1970s.

All of that translated to extra hours of practice for the Wylie Pirates in the days leading up to the showdown with Childress.

"(Coach Shaffer) was concerned about the Childress game, and whether or not we were ready for it," Ronnie Cross remembered. "We worked really hard that week, to the point where guys were like, 'This is crazy.' I can remember getting home at 8, 8:30 at night."

The extra work paid off. On that freezing cold Saturday night against the Bobcats, the Pirates were red hot on both sides of the ball. The offense mounted a second-half rally to put the game out of reach while the defense picked off Childress quarterback Perry Morren five times (three by Tony Garner, one by Roy

McClendon and one by Bruce Cryer). The Bobcats also fumbled it away three times (Tony Garner, Mark Whitehead and Roy McClendon had recoveries for Wylie) for a total of eight turnovers on the night.

"All I had heard all week long was that Childress said they could throw against us," strong safety Tony Garner recalled. "For me, I was excited because there was another opportunity."

And he had plenty of them, mostly because of the usually thorough preparation of Coach Shaffer and the Wylie coaching staff. According to Tony, because of the coaches' extensive preparation, "When they lined up, you knew just about whether it was a pass or not. All it was, was a matter of watching the quarterback…By the time we put the play off, we'd all looked at each other and knew what we were going to do and didn't even have to call anything."

The Pirates proved many times during the season that teams could not turn the ball over that many times against them and expect to win. As was their custom, they seemed to capitalize on every mistake Childress made offensively.

Defensively, the Bobcats were similar to Wylie in that they hit hard and always swarmed around the ball. In fact, Ronnie Cross recalled that the hardest he had ever been hit as the Pirates quarterback was in that Childress game.

"Those guys, man, that was one of the toughest games, physically," Rickey Blackman remembered. "They ran a variation of the wing offense, so I had one guy line up that I lined up on every time…I think I spent all night on one guy, just either him beating me up or me beating him up…typically, that was probably one of the tougher games just because of the style of the strong side linebacker that I was asked to play."

The cold weather was virtually a non-factor in this one for Wylie, very different from the regional game against Bowie the year before in which the weather suddenly turned cold at halftime and the Pirates were unprepared. This time, against Childress, the Pirates were ready for the bitter cold.

Some of the players relied on good old ingenuity to battle the frigid air—they had their mothers sew white bath towels onto their mesh jerseys so they would have a place to keep their hands warm in between plays. One of those players who tried this was Tony Garner—and it worked fabulously.

Other players used other methods to combat the cold. But one thing was certain—the Pirate players and coaches were ready for the weather this time.

"The very first series, I remember my hands being cold," Ronnie Cross recalled. "By about that seventh or eighth snap, it just felt like the football was shattering your hands as it hit it. It was so cold out there. But I came off the sideline, and Coach Shaffer had a guy there that had these mittens on up to his elbows. Every time I'd come off the field, he'd give me those mittens, and my hands never got cold the rest of that ballgame."

In the first quarter, Tony Garner had his first of three interceptions to set Wylie up at the Childress 13. After a clipping penalty moved the Pirates back to the 28, they took four plays to reach the end zone—on an eight yard run by Wayne Mayberry, who finished the evening with 73 yards on 10 carries. Rock King split the uprights and the Pirates led, 7-0. The Pirates controlled the clock in the second quarter but could not get into the end zone, and they took that seven-point lead to the locker room.

Early in the third quarter, Childress was able to tie the score by taking advantage of a Wylie mistake. The Pirates fumbled deep in their own territory, and Ricky Anderson recovered for Childress. Jim Eason crossed the goal line two plays later and Kenny Dean added the PAT to knot the game at 7-all.

Rock King kicked a 32-yard field goal to break the tie later in the third quarter, and the Pirates never gave up the lead after that. After Mark Whitehead recovered a Childress fumble on the Bobcats' next possession, the Pirates padded their lead with two and half minutes left in the third period with a 15-yard touchdown run by Ronnie Cross using the option play.

Then, with 8:36 left in the game, Rock drilled one through the uprights again for three to give the Pirates a 20-7 lead. The Bobcats drove the length of the field on their next possession but Wylie snuffed out the rally when Tony Garner intercepted Perry Morren's pass in the end zone.

This time it was the Pirates' turn to drive all the way, and when they reached the Bobcat nine yard line with less than a minute to play, Rock's 26-yard field goal attempt sailed wide left. On the next play, which was the first play of a Childress drive, middle linebacker Bruce Cryer added the exclamation point for Wylie when he intercepted Morren's pass (intended for Nicky Hardison) and ran it in for the score from 12 yards out with just 28 seconds left. Bruce's touchdown and Rock's ensuing PAT gave the Pirates a 27-7 lead, which is where the score stood when time ran out.

"I just gambled on that play," Bruce said of his interception return for a TD. "I felt like we had it pretty well under control. And we were looking for the pass play, too."

Wylie had played particularly well on defense; their heroes were many. Names like Morgan, Blackman, Schultz, McClendon, Whitehead, Garner, Edge, Cryer and Croley, to name a few, combined to stifle the Bobcats' offense. In addition to forcing eight turnovers, the Pirates' "D" limited Childress to a mere 61 yards rushing in the second half.

The Wylie Pirates had done it again. They had beaten the odds and knocked off another team that was supposed to win easily; a team that had visited the state championship game in each of the previous two years. The Pirates had sent Childress home with another disappointing playoff defeat.

"It was one of those things were everything went our way," Rock King recalled. "Early on, we got most of the breaks. They didn't. It ended up being a pretty easy win. They just didn't give themselves a chance."

The Childress turnovers had been costly to that team, but perhaps just as costly was the Bobcats' lack of preparation for Wylie's running game. The game films Childress studied of Wylie indicated that the Pirates relied heavily on the pass—after all, Ronnie Cross was coming off his best passing game of the season (against Mount Vernon)—hence Childress focused more on preparing to defend the pass than the run.

Coach Shaffer noticed early on in the game that the Bobcats were double-covering the flanker, sending the message that they were expecting the pass. This opened the door for Wylie to run the football more often than they normally would have. As a result, the Pirates burned them for 231 rushing yards—83 each for Ronnie Cross and Wendell Collins and 73 for Wayne Mayberry.

The win advanced the Pirates to the state championship for the first time in their long history. The offense was providing plenty of fireworks, but as the cliché goes, defense wins championships. And the Pirate defense was on its way to doing exactly that.

The following poem was written by three Pirate football players—Chuck Edge, Garth Touchstone and Chris Winters—the week before the team played the state championship game. It was distributed in *The Galleon*, a Wylie High School publication, on Monday, December 19, 1977, two days after the Pirates won the state crown.

> *"We kicked Diamond Hill around,*
> *And they left town with a frown.*
>
> *Kaufman and Farmersville had Peely and Shinn,*
> *And we just couldn't come up with a win.*
>
> *Though Northwest came ready to play,*
> *It just didn't turn out to be their day.*

State Semifinal Playoff, Wylie vs. Childress

We took on the Longhorns, who were ready to ramble,
We taught them not to blitz and gamble!

Midlothian had speed, and we had the "Power,"
And we ranked supreme in our finest hour.

As big "Z" ran against our great wall,
It was in the stars that Allen would fall.

The massacre at Red Oak
Was nothing more than a joke.

Though the Jackrabbits thought they were bad,
After the game, they knew they had been had.

Though the field at Ferris felt like concrete,
The victory still tasted sweet.

Granbury thought they had the game won,
But there were still 32 seconds on the clock to be run.

A pass in the end zone with one second to go
Filled the Breckenridge fans with very much woe.

Though the Mount Vernon Tigers tried in vain,
After the game, they felt only pain.

We faced Childress, a team much like ours.
After the game, they were crying in the showers.

Now that we've made the state playoff game,
Others will know the great Wylie name."

Only one thing stood between Wylie and the Class 2A state championship. It was a huge Goliath named Bellville.

State Championship, Wylie vs. Bellville

The Bellville Brahmas, like Wylie, were gunning for the first state championship in their school's history. They had been to the championship game once before—17 years earlier, in 1960—but lost the title to Denver City.

Unlike Wylie, Bellville had not been the underdogs all season and had more than handily beaten most of their opponents in 1977.

"We were always the underdogs, so we weren't expected to win," Jack Hirmon said. "We weren't really cocky. We didn't talk a lot of trash. We just kind of went out and did our job the way we were trained to do it. We played every game like we had nothing to lose, because we didn't. We weren't supposed to be there, anyway."

The Brahmas entered the state championship game with a 14-0 record. They had outscored opponents in those 14 games, 489-78, meaning they had won each game by an average score of 35-5. Most of the points against Bellville had come in the playoffs; opponents scored only 28 points against the Brahmas in 10 regular season games. They shut out the opponent six times in 14 games, including four in a row at one point.

In the state semifinal, the Brahmas played their closest game of the season, knocking off Yoakum by a 25-19 score.

This Bellville team could run the football. And they were much larger and quicker than Wylie. The defense was led by an all-state linebacker, Paul Albert, who stood at 6-1 and weighed 215, which was as large a linebacker as there was at the 2A level at that time. Another linebacker, Joe Pettiette, was equally large at 6-1, 212. Pettiette and Albert were heavily courted by several schools in the now-defunct Southwest Conference, which at the time included Southern Methodist, Texas Christian, Texas Tech, Baylor, Rice, Houston, the University of Texas, Texas Tech, Texas A&M and Arkansas.

Bellville had been the No. 1 Class 2A team in the state, according to the Associated Press, for most of the season. They knocked off the 1976 Class 2A state champions, Rockdale, in the 1977 playoffs rather easily.

Neither the Wylie defense nor the offense could match up to that of Bellville in size or prestige. But the Pirates had something few teams possessed, something the Duke once found in a young colleague in a movie of the same name: true grit. Any doubt about this was dispelled by Danny Schultz, who was determined to play despite suffering from a cold, a separated shoulder and a hyper-extended knee. Wayne Mayberry recalled that Danny had hurt his shoulder so badly that season that he could not lift his arm to reach out and grab anybody.

Danny's playing through all those injuries in the state title game should not have been unexpected to anyone who knew him, since Danny literally never missed a day of school in his life. Legend has it that one day while walking to school, he was hit by a car, but still did not miss school that day. His determination carried over onto the football field.

"He played through all that pain, every down, every game, and never complained," Wayne said. "You'd almost have to tranquilize him to make him go off and rest sometimes. I've never seen anybody that could endure that much pain."

Chuck Edge, who played next to Danny on the defensive line, said, "It was an inspiration to play next to him and know how bad he was feeling and how bad he was hurting, and he seemed to do a great job. To me, that was an amazing thing, because he was beat up. But Danny never missed a day of school, and he wasn't about to miss a game, either."

Danny was not the only one on the team who was banged up. Ronnie Cross suffered a deep thigh bruise in the Childress game, and Garth Touchstone's knee was still hurting from the Granbury game. Tim Pelton was still out with a broken leg. Roy Fuentes suffered a sprained ankle playing a game of touch football at home a couple of days after his two-interception performance against Mount Vernon. Bob Skipwith, the center as well as the deep snapper for field goal attempts and punts, had played most of the season with a chipped bone in the knuckle of his thumb, which proved painful in snapping the ball. Bob also suffered a deep thigh bruise as a result of a hit in the Childress game.

But pain or no pain, it did not matter—these guys were determined to play in that state championship game no matter what.

"After that (Breckenridge) game, we had quite a few people hurting that played the rest of the season," Wayne Mayberry recalled.

The Wylie defense closely resembled the defense of the 1972 Miami Dolphins, which was dubbed the "No Name Defense" for its lack of a true superstar. But all the "No Name Defense" did for Miami that year was help the team win 17 consecutive games, including the Super Bowl over the Washington Redskins, and post the only unbeaten, untied season in NFL history.

Like that group of Miami Dolphins, a superstar was absent from Wylie's defensive squad. But they made big plays, as evidenced by their performances in the regular season and especially in the playoffs. The defense allowed just 11.2 points per game over the 14 games coming in; take away the loss in week two in which Kaufman scored 53 points, and the Pirate defense had allowed an average of just 7.5 points per game in the other 13 games heading into the state championship.

"We just didn't have a stud out there," strong safety Tony Garner said. "I heard Coach Shaffer say years later that we were probably the most even football team he'd ever seen, meaning that we were all laid back—none of us were real high strung—some of us were a little more than others, but we were pretty even keeled. You couldn't rattle us, and that probably made a bigger difference than anything."

While Wylie's passing game had played a big part in the playoff run, the Bellville Brahmas had stomped all of their opponents with the running game. In addition to being larger, they were easily a quicker team than Wylie; the Brahmas had three 1,000-plus yard rushers in quarterback Rusty Parker (son of Bellville head coach Doyle Parker) and running backs Allen Ward and Reese Burger.

In fact, Bellville ran the ball so much, that at least one member of the Wylie secondary, Tony Garner, figured his role in the game would be small.

"Going into that, I think for the most part we were numb, a little bit," Tony described. "Basically, the week of practice was just tendencies. For me, I remember looking back and going, 'Crud, these boys don't throw the ball ever. And if they do, it's nothing but a little button hook to the outside. And I'm not a cornerback.' That was what was going through my mind the whole time: I was gonna be nothing but support."

Allen Ward, one of Bellville's trio of 1,000-yard rushers, was only a sophomore, and Rusty Parker (6-2, 170), like his two teammates Joe Pettiette and Paul Albert, was being pursued by several Southwest Conference schools. The Bellville offense was averaging nearly a 10-yard gain for every offensive play they had run that year. With a speedy backfield like the one Bellville had, they did not need to throw the ball much, if at all, to score mountains of points.

"In pregame, you could almost smell the confidence on 'em," Jack Hirmon said of Bellville. "You could just see it. They were confident, they were cocky…We're out there sweating our butts off in full pads and they're out there in shimmel shirts. I thought we were playing the University of Texas because of the (uniform) colors and the size of the guys. They were so huge."

"The only game where we really honestly thought we were gonna be totally outmanned was Bellville," Tony Garner stated. "We knew Funderburg (of Breckenridge) and all those guys were huge, but there was only one or two of 'em. Bellville looked like an all-star team. I think Bellville was probably the one team that for us it was like, 'Oh my gosh, what are we gonna do with these guys?'"

The Wylie coaching staff had the answer to that question. They were not going to beat the Brahmas at their own game, so they would have to try something different.

"When we looked at Breckenridge, and then again when we came up against Bellville, from watching them before and during our game preparation, it was like, you understood that you might get blown out in that ballgame," Coach Bruce King said. "I mean, they were physically talented enough that you can see where they might just line up and run over you, and you wouldn't be able to even slow 'em down enough to get in the game.

"In the very first session, we were throwing stuff up on the blackboard that was way out there, because we just knew we couldn't stop 'em under ordinary circumstances."

Despite the seemingly overwhelming task that lay in front of them, the Wylie players were not intimidated by the state's No. 1-ranked team. The Pirates were there to win. While the press or the oddsmakers may have chosen Wylie as the underdogs to Bellville, the Pirates did not consider themselves as such.

"We had gone further than any other team in the history of Wylie," Roy Fuentes recalled. "We had overcome so many odds to get that far, anyway. We were by no means going to be satisfied with just getting there…we definitely went there with the intention of winning the game."

Momentum was critical, according to Jess Croley. "Once we got to rolling, I felt like there wasn't anybody that could beat us," Jess said. "I was pretty confident. Now that the years go on, and the memories fade, we're even better than I thought we were back then."

This Bellville team had played with heavy hearts all season. One of their teammates, Mike McKesska—considered to be one of the best cornerbacks in the state—was killed in an auto accident in the spring of 1977.

The winner of the 1977 Class 2A state title would be decided on the afternoon of December 17 at Baylor Stadium in Waco, in front of about 10,000 crazed football fans. The crowd seemingly included the whole town of Wylie, and everyone on the Pirates' side of the bleachers was chanting "AHMO!" and waving Jolly Roger flags that popped in the wind.

"I think everybody that could make it made it," said Glynn Tyson, Wayne Tyson's younger brother, who was a sophomore that year.

It did not take long for the Brahmas to make a play. They returned the opening kickoff deep into Wylie territory before stepping out of bounds, which was the only thing that prevented a touchdown on the play.

"That was kind of an eye-opener to us as to how much speed they had," Pirate linebacker Rickey Blackman said.

Though Bellville had made the play on the kickoff, it was the Wylie Pirates who struck first, and it was all set up by a big defensive play. It happened because the Brahmas did something the Pirates were not expecting them to do—they challenged the Wylie secondary. Coach Shaffer said because of Wylie's obvious size and speed disadvantages, "There was no way we could contain their option the conventional way, which meant we had to gamble. There were times when we just had to guess based on down, distance, position on the field, their tendencies."

On this particular first quarter play, Coach Shaffer gambled that Bellville would not throw the ball, so he called for a "double corner crash," a play in which the cornerbacks, Dale Morgan and Roy Fuentes, blitz the quarterback and one safety is left back in the secondary—just as a precautionary measure in case a pass is thrown. The double corner crash was designed to put more defenders on the line of scrimmage, according to Coach King, since the Wylie coaches believed it would take two or more of the Pirates to tackle one of the Brahmas because of their size.

All of Bellville's receivers were open on that play, but because of the pressure of the cornerbacks coming from both sides, Rusty Parker hurried his pass, which found its way into the hands of Wayne Mayberry—the safety who had stayed back on that play just in case. Wayne sprinted 90 yards to the Bellville five to put Wylie in a prime position to take an early lead.

"We'd been practicing their offense while we were on defense," Wayne recalled. "There wasn't much field to actually have to cover. Tony (Garner) had to go the strong side and I was on the weak side for safety measures. They hiked the ball, and I'm looking over there and I'm seeing that there's no running play, so I'm just kind of falling back a little bit from watching the quarterback. All that time I sat there and watched him never take his eyes off that receiver and just throw it. Basically, all I did was just step in front of him and run up the sideline with it."

That play also said it all about how much more speed Bellville had. After racing up the sideline nearly the length of the field, Wayne was caught from behind by a Bellville offensive guard who had been pursuing him relentlessly.

"I caught a lot of flack for that," Wayne said with a smile. Then, on a serious note of that play, he said, "I can still see the faces of those players and a coach and a photographer that was down there taking pictures as I ran by there. They couldn't believe it. They'd gotten down there that far and I picked that ball off and was running down through there."

Wayne's interception proved to be huge for Wylie in terms of grabbing early momentum.

"Emotionally, that really took something out of them, it seemed like, and/or added something to us," secondary coach Bruce King said. "That end was going to run into such wide open field that (Parker) just kind of lofted that ball, and Wayne had to come from a long way from where he was to all the way across. That's what we had him doing on that particular play. That was just an all-out gamble, and we're just lucky that it turned out like it did. (Wayne) just made the play and did what he had to do.

"You wouldn't want to have to try to cover that situation like that more than once. But it's kind of like that touchdown play against Breckenridge. It did happen, and that's the way it went down. That was certainly a turning point in that whole ballgame, because if I remember correctly, I don't remember them lining up and running the ball over us the rest of that ballgame."

The Wylie drive following Wayne's interception began with a four-yard loss. On the second play, Ronnie Cross connected with Doug Gollahon for a nine-yard touchdown and Rock King kicked the PAT for a 7-0 Wylie lead with 4:18 remaining in the first period.

Bellville had the size and speed to play conventional football, but was unable to adjust to Wylie's unconventional ways, especially their red zone offense. The Pirates had lined up with no one in their backfield and Ronnie found his tight end wide open in the end zone for Wylie's first touchdown. "It was like playing catch. It was that simple," Coach Shaffer described. "Even though we're not fast, they've got to be where we are. They can't run as fast as the ball travels through the air. That's the one thing that slow people have still going for them—no matter how fast the other guys are, they aren't as fast as a forward pass."

The Brahmas were not used to trailing, so they came back quickly. Before the end of the first quarter, Bellville answered with a 46-yard touchdown run from another one of their speedsters, John Jackson. The Brahmas made the two-point conversion to take a one-point lead at 8-7.

Bellville was not prepared for what Wylie had to give them next. About halfway through the second quarter, Coach Shaffer called for an option pass with Rock King lined up at tight end and Doug Gollahon lined up at halfback.

From Bellville's point of view, first the play seemed to be a counter-option to Doug, but the handoff went to Rock, and then play appeared to be an end-around. But Rock—who, outside of an unsuccessful fake punt attempt against Breckenridge and a couple of times at the end of the Mount Vernon state quarterfinal, had not thrown a pass in a game situation since the Forney game more than a month prior—spotted Doug wide open and threw a strike to him for a 42-yard touchdown. Coach Shaffer had shown this play to Rock a few days earlier in an Algebra class and told Rock that the Pirates would score a touchdown against Bellville using this play.

"They bit on that," Doug explained. "It looked like a running play, then it looked like an end-around reverse. We worked on that play, I know for sure, four weeks before we used it. We never used it in any of the games until that game."

According to Rock, "Ronnie faked the veer one direction, I played tight end and came around the other direction, and Doug was the halfback and he came out. He went all the way downfield, and he was wide open. He was probably behind the guy 20 yards…I remember being scared I was gonna overthrow him or underthrow him, he was so wide open. It wasn't something where we had to thread the needle. I just had to step back and throw it up in the air.

"Doug had to wait on it a long time. Of course, it probably seemed like an eternity to him. Actually, the guy that was on the coverage had time to make an adjustment to almost be able to tackle Doug before he got into the end zone. But again, Doug made a good play and got into the end zone."

The Pirates lined up to kick the PAT, but Coach Shaffer called for a fake, and Ronnie and Doug hooked up again for the two-point conversion to make the score 15-8 in favor of Wylie with 6:47 left in the first half.

But before halftime, Rusty Parker's 35-yard touchdown gallop on a fourth and two play put Bellville in a position to tie it up. The Brahmas chose to go for two rather than kick the point, however. A successful two-point conversion at that point would put the Brahmas in the lead by one point.

Much like the final play at Breckenridge, this is where being well-coached paid off for the Pirates. Coach Page had done all the studying on Bellville's tendencies and discovered that the Brahmas had two main running plays they liked to use, especially in short yardage situations—the outside veer and the quick pitch. Coach Page gambled that Bellville would call the quick pitch and he had his defense line up using the same formation as they used against Breckenridge—the one where the linebacker lined up against the defensive tackle and looped around.

If Bellville used the outside veer, this defensive scheme would not work. It was guaranteed to stop the quick pitch, however. As the coaches discussed on the sideline which play to use, Coach Shaffer believed Bellville would run the outside veer and thought the Pirates should use a different defensive scheme.

"I told him, 'They're going to run the quick pitch,'" Coach Page recalled. "And he said, 'Okay, Rick. You've been studying them. You've got the call.' Sure enough, they ran the quick pitch."

Largely as a result of Coach Page's preparation, Rickey Blackman, Jess Croley and Danny Schultz—separated shoulder and all—stopped Rusty Parker short of the goal line on the two-point attempt. It was a play that turned out to be a momentum killer for Bellville, since Wylie retained the lead by stopping the Brahmas on that two-point attempt. Guessing correctly on this play later proved to be one of Rick Page's proudest moments as a defensive coordinator.

"I think they instilled the fact that if you know what they're gonna do, you'll be looking for it," Jess explained. "Most of the time, they did what he said they were gonna do."

After a Wylie punt, Bellville moved the ball to the Pirate eight with a pass from Rusty Parker to Gary Travis. After an illegal motion penalty pushed the Brahmas back five yards, Steve Jackson had a shot at putting Bellville up by two at halftime. But his 30-yard field goal attempt sailed wide right, and Bellville trailed by a point at 15-14 heading into the locker room. It was the first time all season they found themselves on the short end at halftime.

Jack Hirmon recalled: "I think we knew we were going to win at halftime. In fact, the coaches reiterated when we went in at halftime that (Bellville) had never been behind at halftime. It was time to finish it out, and of course, we went out there and did it…I don't think they thought they could be beat. I think after halftime, they panicked and found out that they could be beat."

At halftime, Coach King asked the members of his secondary what coverage they would prefer to use against Bellville for the second half. Based on having played against the Brahmas' offense for one half, each member of the Wylie secondary knew exactly what he wanted to do.

"All of them agreed, 'We want to do this,' which was more of our basic zone coverage type situation," Coach King explained. "I said, 'Okay, that's what we're going to stay in, then. It's your call, and if you can get it done like that, that's what we want to do.' I can remember thinking back afterward how that moment was one of the most gratifying things to be a part of, because you saw how those guys had matured and just how that kind of a relationship that you have had turned around completely from what it was, say, toward the end of the third week of that season (against Farmersville)."

In their second possession of the third quarter, the Pirates drove deep in to Brahma territory—helped out by the inside running of Wayne Mayberry, Tony Garner and Ronnie Cross—before Reese Burger intercepted Ronnie's pass in the end zone and returned it 53 yards to midfield. Trailing by only a point, Bellville had an excellent chance to take the lead. But the drive ended when Gary Travis fumbled after catching a halfback pass and Rickey Blackman recovered at the Pirate 22 yard line.

"They threw a pass, and it was pretty far down the field," Rickey remembered. "I was pretty fast, and I had pretty good drop coverage on the play. So I went back and kind of caught the guy from behind as he was making a move. Somebody had spiked the ball and the ball fell out, and I actually ended up recovering the fumble. I remember that, in my mind, was a pretty big play. It was the second half, and it was such a close game. Any turnovers at that point were pretty critical, so that helped us out."

Indeed, it did help the Pirates. Following the fumble recovery, they mounted an 11-play, 78-yard touchdown drive to go up by eight. Aided by a 20-yard completion from Ronnie Cross to Roy Fuentes and a 31-yard pass play from Ronnie to Wayne Tyson, the Pirates had the ball at the Brahma 19 and found themselves in a position to score again. After moving the ball to the 12, Ronnie found Roy Fuentes open in the end zone for the touchdown with 3:03 left in the third quarter. Roy had been left uncovered due to the monstrous pass rush of Bellville, which hit Ronnie almost immediately after he threw the ball. Rock King kicked the point for a 22-14 lead.

According to Roy Fuentes, that was the third time in a row the Pirates had run that play, and the third time was a charm. "It was like a post route, and we just straightened it out a little bit," Roy said of that touchdown play. "The defensive back was playing more toward the center. It was a good throw, and it was right there."

Just as the Pirate defense had done all season, but particularly in the playoffs, Wylie forced two crucial second-half turnovers to stop Bellville drives. With less than a minute to play in the third quarter, the Brahmas drove it to the Wylie 12 when Danny Schultz jarred the ball loose from Allen Ward. Defensive tackle Mike Helm recovered at the Wylie nine.

Wylie could not do anything with this turnover, however. A few plays later, Rock King was forced to punt from his own end zone, and he drilled a 47-yarder.

A few minutes later, he punted again, but this time had to field a low snap and punt while trying to escape the rush. The result was a nine-yarder that gave Bellville the ball at the their own 39.

The Wylie defense forcing turnovers and making crucial plays was one of the things that led to the Pirates' offense controlling of the clock in the second half, thus keeping the Bellville defense on the field for extended periods of time and wearing them down.

Time was running out on Bellville. They needed a touchdown and a two-point conversion to tie it, and with the speed they possessed, it would only take only one play if they could get around one of the ends.

But it never happened. The Wylie defense simply would not allow it.

"We just knew what we had to do," defensive end Jess Croley said. "The main thing was don't let 'em get outside. Just do our job, really, was all we stressed. We all knew what we had to do, and we did it as a team, and that's why it happened."

Late in the fourth quarter, the Brahmas drove into Pirate territory. But that Pirate defense was there again to make the stop.

On third down, linebacker Rickey Blackman came up with a big sack of Rusty Parker. "We called a blitz, and we didn't blitz that often," Rickey recalled. "I was fortunate enough to be in the right place at the right time, and I made a big sack."

The Brahmas went for it on fourth down, and cornerback Dale Morgan picked off Rusty Parker's pass at the Wylie eight.

The Pirates began to run out the clock, but with just under two minutes left, their lead appeared to be in jeopardy when Ronnie Cross lost the ball and a Bellville defender caught it in the air and darted toward the end zone. The officials ruled that Ronnie was down before he fumbled, however.

Granted a reprieve, Ronnie stepped up and made the big play on third and 18. He ran for a 29-yard gain for a first down that all but won the first state championship in Wylie's history. The frustration of losing had finally taken a toll at least one of Bellville's defensive players, who leveled Wylie's center, Bob Skipwith, from behind after the play was dead.

"He cleaned my clock…he just sent me rolling. He wasn't penalized, or anything. I guess it went undetected, but I sure felt it," Bob recalled. "We exchanged some words after I got up, and we went on our merry ways."

With a new set of downs and 1:22 remaining, Wylie could simply fall on the ball. Ronnie took a knee to run out the clock and the Pirates had beaten the No. 1 team in the state by the score of 22-14. Against all odds, Wylie had captured the 1977 Texas Class 2A football state title. It was theirs and no one could take it away from them.

Pirate fans flooded the field to celebrate to form a scene Jack Hirmon described as "mass bedlam." Generations came together as the Wylie players greeted the enthusiastic throng of fans, many of whom were former Pirate players who had never made it to that point in their high school football careers.

"It was pretty wild," Jess Croley said of the scene on the field after the Pirates won. "There were a lot of happy people there, a lot of family, a lot of friends, people rushing on the field and all…I knew it was something that hadn't been done before, and they stressed that to us—the history, and all."

Ronnie Cross remembered the post-game celebration on the field. "Really, the greatest thing about the whole thing after it was all over was seeing my dad on the field, and all those guys that played at Wylie before us. That was the biggest thing, is that all the people that never had that opportunity. And yet, here we were, lucky enough to be there and win the whole thing."

This was a moment especially cherished by the seniors, nearly all of which had played football with or against each other since the fourth grade. And not just football—many of them had played baseball and basketball and run track together. They had practiced football for countless hours together since the start of two-a-days in August and had also spent many hours together off the football field over the years.

One of those seniors, Wayne Mayberry, said his favorite memory of that 1977 season was, "Actually realizing that you won state, and realizing that this was the last game you were going to play, and having photographers and interviewers all on the field, and having the whole town out there…that was pretty special."

In the playoffs, Ronnie had really mastered the veer offense. He gained huge chunks of yardage by repeatedly following the halfback outside, faking a pitch and tucking the ball at the last second, thus tricking the opponent into thinking that the halfback had the ball. Sometimes, the halfback paid for it. But often, by the time the other team figured out what was going on, Ronnie was off to the races.

For the Bellville game, Ronnie recalled specifically that the Pirates repeatedly used the veer offense to run a counter-option play which they had seldom run in the 14 games prior. Using the counter-option, the Pirates would fake moving the ball to the strong side, freeze the linebackers—particularly Paul Albert, the middle linebacker, whom they keyed in on—and at the last second reverse field and run the ball to the weak side. Bellville was not prepared for this play most of the time.

"We'd play off the misdirection," center Bob Skipwith explained. "Try to get (Albert) moving one way, then when he figured out he was going the wrong way and came back, we'd have somebody in his face to take him down, basically…A lot of misdirection plays to try to freeze him so that he couldn't pursue as quickly or actually try to get him going the wrong direction."

The Pirate defense had shut out Bellville in the second half, marking the first time all season the Brahmas had been held scoreless for an entire half. In fact, Wylie dominated the second half in nearly all facets of the game, but particularly with the offensive line.

The Brahmas rushed for 310 yards in the game, but they gained only 94 of those yards in the second half after the Wylie defense had really clamped down. Passing-wise, Rusty Parker was good on five of nine for 73 yards but with two critical interceptions. In fact, Bellville turned the ball over to Wylie five times, and nearly every one was costly to the Brahmas. By comparison, Wylie's offense committed three turnovers (one interception, two fumbles) to give them a plus two in that category.

"The big thing about that game is our defense was unbelievable," Rock King explained. "Wayne Mayberry had a big interception. They were moving the ball and getting ready to score, and if they'd have punched that in the end zone, I don't know if we'd have been able to come back. That was a huge turnaround. We made some defensive adjustments and took some risks on defense because they were so physically dominating. In coverages, we brought cornerbacks that we never would have done in the regular scheme, and made some big adjustments, and it worked out."

Childress, Bellville and several others that season proved that even the best football teams simply could not afford to turn the ball over to Wylie, because more often than not, the Pirates would make them pay.

Coach Page remembered the Breckenridge and Bellville playoff games as his favorite, from a defensive coordinator standpoint as well as from an offensive line standpoint, since the Pirates were able to shut down two fast, strong, high-powered offenses as well as two physical, bruising defenses. "For us to do that in those two games—to stop people with that kind of talent—was really impressive to me," he said.

The Wylie Pirates had overcome many opponents both in the playoff and in district play that were superior in both size and speed. And they did it using finesse, just as Coach Shaffer had said.

"We were at a gross disadvantage size-wise," Bob Skipwith remembered. "It was always an area of concern, because you think, big/size/strength/the guy's hard to move. But we were dedicated, we were focused and we worked on those quick three steps out of our stance and tried to get position. Then we'd try to use leverage to get 'em where we wanted 'em to go, or at least tie 'em up long enough to give the backs a chance to get through or to give Ronnie or Rock time to get the pass off. It worked pretty well, as the record shows."

The Pirates celebrated their state title by eating at a Waco dinery before heading home. When the bus rolled into Pirate Stadium just before 10 o'clock on December 17, a throng of ecstatic Wylie fans waited there to greet them. In the crowd were many Plano football fans, who earlier that day had watched their team wrap up the Class 4A state championship, 13-10, over Port Neches-Grove at Texas Stadium in Irving. One of the local newspapers reported that the Plano fans at Texas Stadium erupted into cheers for their Collin County neighbors when the final score of the Wylie-Bellville game was announced.

Like Wylie, Plano was known for being a well-coached team, first by John Clark in the late 60s and the first half of the 70s, then by Tom Kimbrough in the late 70s and throughout the 80s. When Plano won the title in 1977, it was Kimbrough's second year as the Wildcats' coach.

Plano also developed several players who took their football careers to the next level. One of those was Billy Ray Smith, who played on the 1977 state champion Plano team. Billy Ray went on to a College Hall of Fame career with the University of Arkansas and a standout career in the NFL with the San Diego Chargers from 1983–92.

Plano had been to the big one and won it before. In fact, their 1977 title was their fourth in 12 years. But for Wylie, this was something new, something the kids never dreamed of experiencing.

"With us doing it and Plano doing it at the same time, it was almost like a little brother-big brother type thing," Roy Fuentes recalled. "You have the big brother, Plano, that was over there marching through the state playoffs, and we were the little brother doing it. We were rooting for them, and they were rooting for us, and we were both maroon. It was just meant to be, I guess."

Wylie and Plano had achieved one of the rarest of high school football feats by winning the state title in 1977. Two teams from the same county capturing the state title in the same year had happened only twice in Texas high school football history before 1977—in 1969 with Wichita Falls and Iowa Park of Wichita County, and in 1973 with Tyler John Tyler and Troup of Smith County (that 1973 Tyler John Tyler team featured a future NFL Hall of Fame running back named Earl Campbell).

Collin County actually had a chance to boast three state champions in 1977. Wylie's neighbors up the road, Farmersville, finished as the champions of District 15-A. The Farmers won the bi-district game against Cooper, 14-7, but lost to Pottsboro for the regional championship, 14-6. From there on out, the Farmersville players who were friends with the Wylie players followed the Pirates' progress in the playoffs.

"I think it was a little surprising they did as well as they did," Farmersville quarterback Bobby Bishop said of the 1977 Pirates. "They really came together as a team. Coach Shaffer did a great job. At the time (Farmersville beat Wylie in week three), it wasn't as big as a deal as it became later when they won the state championship. I don't think at the time we really realized what we had done."

The Wylie High School football team had given their fans a good reason to celebrate—out of 218 teams that began the season in Class 2A in Texas in 1977, Wylie was the only one left standing at the end. The Pirates had reached the pinnacle, and both the players and the people of Wylie wanted to savor the moment together at the stadium in Wylie the night of December 17.

Tony Garner had a simple theory as to why the Pirates were able to defeat the state's No. 1 team to win the title: "I think we played like we played all year long. We played as a unit, not as 11 individuals."

"If we played Bellville 10 times, realistically, we might have won that one," Ronnie Cross stated. "If we played Breckenridge 10 times, realistically, we might have won that one. If we played Childress 10 times, we might have won that one. We beat the top three teams in the state that year, so to say that we weren't the best team in the state of Texas that particular year—that would be a bald-faced lie, because we were. On the day we lined up to play 'em, we did what we needed to do to beat 'em. I think that's what separates that particular team from any other team that's ever come out of Wylie. We've had a lot of great teams and we've had more talented teams come out than what we were, by far. You just take the quarterback position. There's been a heck of a lot of 'em better than what I was. But we were able to get it done, and that's the greatest part of that whole thing. We all did it together, and there wasn't one of us any better than the other one. None of us thought that. It was just a team effort.

"We were all just one big family, that group of guys," Ronnie continued. "That's the part that's really the most special, is that we all did it together and we all weren't supposed to."

Postseason Awards

In the days and weeks after December 17, 1977, Collin County was still buzzing about two of their schools winning the state title. The Collin County commissioners requested team photos for both Plano and Wylie for display in the county courthouse. The commissioners called an emergency meeting the weekend after Wylie and Plano won the titles, and at that meeting the commissioners passed a resolution to declare Collin County as the High School Football Capital of The State of Texas.

A state championship and a 13-2 record will generally turn some heads, and the Wylie Pirates did just that in 1977. When it came time for the All-District 12-2A voting, the district's coaches voted four Wylie players on the first team offense, four on the first team defense, four on the second team offense and two on the second team offense. Coaches were allowed to nominate players on their own teams but were not permitted to vote for them.

Wylie Pirates on the first team offense included Ronnie Cross at quarterback, Garth Touchstone and Doug Gollahon at tight end and Phil Lemons at offensive tackle. Pirates on the second team offense were Wayne Mayberry at running back, Tony Garner at flanker, Lon Wallace at offensive right guard and Bob Skipwith at center. An honorable mention for offensive play went to Wendell Collins at running back.

Defense is what carried the Wylie Pirates through district play and the playoffs—through 12 consecutive wins—after the loss to Farmersville in the third game of the season.

"Our defense was the key to our whole success, when you get right down to it," Ronnie Cross said. "Our defense was always in it for us, and they always put us in a position to win the ballgame and kept us in that position."

Opposing coaches in District 12-2A took notice of Wylie's defense—four Pirates made first team defense. The coaches voted defensive tackle Chuck Edge and defensive end Jess Croley to the first team defense along with cornerback Roy Fuentes and safety Tony Garner, who led the world in interceptions with 23. In fact, at the time, that number was a single season record for Texas high school football (it was tied two years later by Kendall Barrow of High Island, a Class A school).

Combined with the 19 interceptions he had in 1976 as a junior, Tony finished his high school football career with 42 pickoffs in just 27 games played. That total of 42 interceptions ranks him third all-time among Texas high school football players; only Donald Moore of 3A Splendora with 59 (1976–79) and Jim Linnstaeder of 4A Brenham with 55 (1956–58) have more career interceptions on the gridiron in Texas than Tony Garner.

His knack for being where the ball was thrown should not have come as a surprise to anyone who had been watching him play all those years growing up in Wylie; interceptions just seemed to come naturally to Tony.

"Ronnie Cross used to live next door to me, and even as a kid, I'd get five or six interceptions just playing around," Tony said. "Even today, playing basketball, I can go out there and steal 10 balls out of two hours worth of basketball."

According to Tony, one of the reasons he had so many interceptions in his high school career was the Pirates' ability to consistently get ahead of opponents. "We would get up by two touchdowns on somebody," Tony explained, "and what are they gonna do? They're gonna chunk it deep."

Second team all-district defensive players from Wylie were defensive end Danny Schultz and linebacker Rickey Blackman. Honorable mentions for defense went to defensive tackle Tim Pelton, linebacker Mark Whitehead, safety Wayne Mayberry and cornerback Dale Morgan.

But the superlatives are where the 12-2A coaches really gave Wylie the respect. Wylie took home the honors of Offensive Player of the Year (tight end Doug Gollahon), Defensive Player of the Year (defensive end Jess Croley), the district's Kicking Specialist of the Year (Rock King) and Coach of the Year (Jerry Shaffer).

When it came to the Texas Sportswriters Association's vote for the all-state team, Wylie did not receive near as much respect as they did from the coaches in their own district. Tight end Doug "Fudgie" Gollahon was voted to first team all-state, the only Wylie player voted to either the first team or second team.

"It was quite an honor. I was really surprised," Doug said of his all-state selection. "We had to get deep into the playoffs, typically, to get that kind of recognition unless your stats are just outstanding."

Some familiar Wylie opponents dotted the list of the TSA all-state team. The first team offense included guard Joe Pettiette, tackle Paul Albert and quarterback Rusty Parker, all from Bellville. Albert also made the first team defense as a linebacker, and Kenny Dean of Childress was voted to the first team as a placekicker. A 6-3, 200-pound junior running back from Sealy named Eric Dickerson—someone who later would figure prominently in spoiling the Pirates' bid to repeat as state champs—was named to the first team offense by the Texas sportswriters.

On the second team defense, Pettiette from Bellville was chosen as a linebacker, and Roger "Peely" Jones from Kaufman ran his way onto the second team offense.

Being counted among names such as those presents an idea of just what kind of a season Doug Gollahon had for Wylie in 1977. For the season, Doug caught 55 passes for 880 yards and 14 touchdowns as a 5-10, 165-pound tight end. His last two touchdowns were the biggest, coming in the state championship against Bellville. In the days before seemingly every high school football team in Texas ran the pass-oriented spread offense, Doug's receiving totals for that year really stood out. In fact, Doug held the single-season records for most receptions and most yards at Wylie High School until Chris Ross surpassed them in 2001 in only 10 games (the next year, in 2002, Ross caught 110 passes, good for third all-time for a single season in Texas).

"For our veer offense, the tight ends were more like fullbacks," Chuck Edge said. "Doug was undersized, but had great hands and ran great routes. Very smart player, very up, very positive, never got down."

Ronnie Cross said of Doug, who eventually became his college roommate at Texas Lutheran University, "He did a lot with the football once he caught the pass. He made you look like a hero a lot of times. He was the one that it goes down as a touchdown pass for 60 yards, but it doesn't tell how he outran everybody for 50 of those yards. He helped us tremendously, and he was the only guy on the team who made all-state, and deservedly so."

"I developed a real good friendship with Ronnie in the short time I was there," Doug explained. "I had confidence in Ronnie throwing the ball, and I think he had confidence that I would catch it."

Doug also had a great relationship with Rock King, since the two had been best friends growing up together in Burleson. Rock and Doug connected for several touchdowns in 1977, largely the result of the two knowing each other so well and having played on several teams together while growing up.

"I knew everything Rock was going to do and when," Doug recalled.

The local daily papers recognized Wylie's state championship season. Doug Gollahon was named to the *Dallas Times Herald*'s All-Metro First Team Offense, and Jerry Shaffer was selected as the All-Metro Coach of the Year by that newspaper (he shared the honor with Coach Tom Kimbrough of Plano). Doug and Coach Shaffer were the only two from Wylie to be honored by the *Times Herald* on the All-Metro Team, though several Pirates received honorable mentions: Ronnie Cross at quarterback, Rock King at place-kicker, Jess Croley at offensive tackle and Tony Garner at safety.

In January 1978, the Wylie Quarterbacks Club sponsored the end of the season banquet for the state champion Pirate team and handed out team awards. Wayne Tyson and Jack Hirmon received the award for being the Most Spirited Players; Paul Adams and Bob Skipwith were named Most Improved Players; Jess Croley was named the team's Outstanding Lineman; Wayne Mayberry and Ronnie Cross were named the Pirates' Outstanding Backs; and the team captains were Ronnie Cross, Jess Croley and Doug Gollahon.

Most members of the 1977 Wylie Pirates did not play college football. Out of the few that did, none played a complete four years, according to Coach Shaffer. Rickey Blackman, who graduated from Wylie High School in the spring of 1979, was courted by some Division I universities but went on to play at Angelo State (a Division II university located in San Angelo, Texas) for two years as a backup safety. Rock King played four years of baseball at Texas A&M as a pitcher and was a team captain for his last two years. He also did some punting for the Aggie football team.

The Pirates' lone all-state representative from the 1977 team, Doug Gollahon, played two years of college football—one at Texas Lutheran University (in Seguin, Texas) and one at Austin College in Sherman, Texas, which happened to be the alma mater of many of the 1977 Wylie coaches.

Coach Shaffer is quick to add that just because no one on the state champion Wylie team became a football superstar in college, "That doesn't mean that they weren't good high school football players."

If anything, it proved the old cliché to be true that the whole is greater than the sum of its parts.

"It was a credit to the team and how hard everybody worked," Rickey Blackman said. "We weren't that big of a team. We might have had a couple of guys that weighed over 200 pounds. I was the strong side linebacker, and I weighed 160, 165 at the time. Our middle probably weighed 180…I don't think there's any kid that you look back and say, 'Wow, that one was a miss. He should have gone on to A&M, or Texas' or someone like that. We just didn't have those kinds of people. We had good, 2A-type football players."

Their Place In History

The 1977 state championship season is imbedded in Wylie history. It can be read plainly on a banner hanging in the locker room of the fabulous IMPAC workout facility, located on campus at Wylie High School right next to the $10.5 million Wylie Pirate Stadium, which opened in 2003. In the first game ever played at the stadium—a junior varsity game on August 28, 2003—the first Pirate touchdown was scored by Chase Foster, the son of former Pirate quarterback Gary Foster, who pitched the ball to Wayne Tyson some 27 years earlier to score the first touchdown in the Pirates' first game at the previous Pirate Stadium.

To this day, when people bring up high school football in Wylie, Jerry Shaffer's name is not far behind. Anytime his name is mentioned around Wylie, it is only a matter of time before the state championship team or the Breckenridge game is discussed. The city of Wylie loves to remember the 14 years Shaffer spent as head coach of the Pirates, but they particularly love to talk about the state championship year of 1977.

Coach Rick Page recalled what a vital role Coach Shaffer had in bringing the state championship to Wylie. He said he believed the citizens of Wylie were aware of that vital role Coach Shaffer played, "but to actually have been a part of that, working with him and seeing how he did things, and how he brought some things on and saw them come to fruition," Coach Page explained. "The vision that he had can never be underestimated. Jerry was a member of my wedding party. I just love the guy, and I think he's just a super, super human being."

Coach Page remembered the play in the state championship where the Pirates stopped Bellville quarterback Rusty Parker on the two-point conversion attempt as a play that epitomized Jerry Shaffer's coaching style. The head coach trusted Coach Page to make the call on that particular play, and Coach Page had guessed correctly as to which offensive scheme Bellville would run.

"Jerry gave us jobs to do, and trusted us to do them," Coach Page said. "In that moment where he could have overruled me, he deferred to my judgment, and it worked."

But what if Coach Page had been wrong, and Bellville had gone with the outside veer instead of the quick pitch?

"I'm 100 percent sure he would have never said anything about that against me," Coach Page said. "That moment, I think, really stands out in two ways. One, it was a high point in my defensive coordinating career, so to speak. The other is a real example of what Jerry Shaffer was like as a head coach to his assistants. It was a wonderful moment that has always been frozen in my memory."

Coaches new to the staff at either Wylie High School or Wylie Junior High School recognized how much Coach Shaffer had to offer. One of those was Jon Peters, who came to WJHS in 1984 as a coach and part of the team that scouted upcoming opponents for the high school football team.

"As a brand new coach, I tried to learn as much as I could," Coach Peters explained, "and Coach Shaffer was more than happy to teach me all that I knew."

On November 8, 2002, Coach Shaffer was on hand for the pre-game coin toss at the final Wylie varsity football game played at Pirate Stadium, the stadium of which he was such an integral part of the construction.

In the summer of 2003, the stadium was renamed Jerry Shaffer Stadium in honor of the former Pirates' coach, and many former Wylie football players were on hand for the celebration. Shaffer Stadium sits on the campus of Grady Burnett Junior High School, which served as Wylie High School from 1976–1996.

In 1996, a new, larger Wylie High School was built a few miles away on FM 544 to accommodate Wylie's rapid growth. Today, Shaffer Stadium is used for Burnett Junior High football games and a host of other junior high school athletic events.

Coach Shaffer and his staff from the 1977 team still command a great deal of respect from those players more than a quarter century after bringing the state title home to Wylie. Just how much respect do they command?

Jack Hirmon summed it up when he said of the celebration in the summer of 2003 after Pirate Stadium was changed to Jerry Shaffer Stadium. "We were at Ronnie Cross's house, and some of us had beers in our hands. We're 40 years old and older…Coach Shaffer and Coach Page come walking in, and there's guys scattering to hide their beers!"

To preserve such an historical season of games, Jack Hirmon—at his own expense—took advantage of modern technology by having all the game films from 1977 professionally converted into VHS videocassettes, then had the videocassettes converted into DVDs (digital video discs). The entire season, including the scrimmages with Seagoville and Princeton, fit on three DVDs.

Much of the quality has been lost from those game films, which sat in the Texas heat of Coach Shaffer's attic for many years. In a few places, the film was completely lost to the heat, particularly in the playoff games that were filmed in color (all of the regular season games and the first two playoff games were filmed in black and white). The films were shot with 16-millimeter movie cameras, before the widespread use of camcorders.

"I thought it was real important to preserve that history for future generations," Jack explained.

"It was a magical season, of course," said Bruce King, who went on to coach the Pirate baseball team to a 17-2-1 record and a regional championship, which was the furthest Class 2A played to at that time (only 3A and 4A played to a state championship prior to 1979). Incidentally, that Pirate baseball team included several members of the state championship football team: Rock King, Doug Gollahon, Ronnie Cross, Jess Croley, Chuck Edge, Rickey Blackman, Bruce Cryer, Dan Whitt, Wendell Collins, Tim Pelton, Robert Martinez and Mike Marshall.

Coach King went out on top, with championships in both baseball and football under his belt. In the summer of 1978, he left coaching to go into plumbing, and he later entered the insurance business. He said of the football championship in Wylie, "It was one of those things that gets kind of burned into your memory—a lot of little instances and circumstances, because of the intensity involved. It was certainly one of the most gratifying times and things that I've ever had the opportunity to be involved in."

On the significance of winning a high school state football championship, Coach Rick Page said, "You feel so fortunate to have ever coached on a state championship team in whatever sport. Just to be fortunate enough to be able to do that is something that will always remain dear to me, and I'll always be in debt to the young men that played on our team to give me that opportunity. It just doesn't happen that much. The longer I've been in the business, the more I realize how special that was."

"I don't think kids nowadays realize what that can do for you," middle linebacker Bruce Cryer said. "It did a lot for me. It builds a drive in you, and that's what carries on after sports. I think going through all those games and all those wins instills something in you. Whatever I did after school, I was going to do 110 percent. I used that same concept we were coached on. It just stays with you. Camaraderie has a lot to do with it. I think everyone on that team had that same drive."

"It was exhilarating," Rock King said of the feeling of winning the state championship. "You see things like that on TV, or whatever, in college games and pro games. But to experience it like that and have a whole town and a community be involved in it…and the whole community was involved in it, not just the school.

Being a small town like that, everybody went to all the games. It was almost surreal in a lot of ways.

"I don't think it soaked in for a long time what we had accomplished as a team," Rock continued. "Being a kid, 16, 17 years old, you think that's the way it's supposed to be. As an adult looking back, you realize how many things had to happen in order for you to get an opportunity like that. There's guys that coach their whole career, play for years and obviously don't ever get a chance to do that. It was a real special time. It was a great feeling, and certainly something that you don't forget."

The City of Wylie, and Wylie High School in particular, recognized the 20th anniversary of that 1977 team with a halftime ceremony at a 1997 home game. Commemorative patches were issued, which the Pirates wore on their uniforms that season.

Many members of the state championship team gathered at Pirate Stadium for that halftime celebration and were introduced to the crowd, which in turn showed its appreciation.

"A state championship is something that no one can ever take away from you," Phil Lemons said. "Coach Shaffer wanted to start a tradition, and I guess the tradition really started when we were freshmen (in the fall of 1974). We were the first to win state, and it doesn't matter how many teams win state from Wylie—we'll always be the first team."

The Legend Of AHMO

AHMO remains an important part of Wylie High School athletics and school spirit. It is printed on everything—football uniforms, basketball uniforms, t-shirts, hats, visors, mugs, towels, thermoses, car windows, head bands, wrist bands, on the gym floor at the high school...wherever one goes in Wylie, especially on the day of a football game, one is bound to see the word AHMO printed, written or shoe polished on something. The word AHMO is seen so many places in Wylie that Coach Shaffer has even called it "ubiquitous."

"I'm surprised that it's actually lasted this long," said Wayne Mayberry, whose son, Cody, began his football career at Wylie High School as a freshman in the fall of 2003. "When they first came up with that, we were all kind of, 'Do we really want to do this?' Evidently, it must have caught on pretty good."

And to think it all started more than a quarter century ago as a result of Coach Shaffer's watching *Dean Martin's Celebrity Roast* in his bedroom after a late football practice.

Those who played football at Wylie High School before 1977 are quick to point out that WHS students had ways of exhibiting pride and school spirit long before AHMO was created. At the same time, no one could deny that the start of AHMO began a new era in Wylie High School's lengthy history.

It is a simple four-letter word, yet it has so much meaning. When someone coming to the town for the first time asks what it means—and they always do—the explanation they are given is that AHMO is an acronym for Annihilate, Humiliate, Mutilate and Obliterate, as in what the Wylie Pirates do to their opponents. Or they explain that it stands for Agile, Hostile, Mobile Offense, which could describe the way the Pirates move the ball.

To Chase Gibson, who played free safety on the 2002 and 2003 Pirate playoff teams, AHMO has so much meaning to the people of Wylie that he would rather not explain it to an outsider who asks him what the word means.

"If they're not from Wylie, I just tell 'em don't worry about it," said Chase, a third generation Wylie Pirate (his father, Benji, played for Wylie in the early 1970s; and Benji's father, Jesse, was a Pirate in the early 1950s. Chase's older brother, Brandon, class of 2002, was also a third generation Pirate).

It is likely that only a small percentage of Wylie High School students and even their parents to some extent are aware of AHMO's origins. Yet they know it means school pride and school spirit for Wylie.

The word has taken on new meaning to some of the Pirate players who were there when it began. Today, when Wayne Mayberry hears the word AHMO, he thinks simply of the "fourth quarter. Time to play the rest of the game like you started the game."

A new chapter in Pirate football history was written on September 5, 2003, when the Wylie Pirates won their first varsity game ever played at the new Wylie Pirate Stadium, 31-0, over Cleburne. In that game, the play of the Pirate defense recalled that of their state champion 1977 counterparts—they limited Cleburne to less than 100 yards of total offense. Michael White scored Wylie's first varsity touchdown at the new stadium.

Just to make sure the Cleburne game was not a fluke, the Pirates beat Commerce rather convincingly, 24-7, the following week in the second varsity game at the new stadium. They finished the 2003 season with a 4-1 record at home, with the only loss coming to Highland Park, 14-3, on Halloween night—which was also the night of the Pirates' homecoming.

Legend has it that there was a movement in Wylie in the late 1980s and early 1990s to remove AHMO. Those who tried to remove it claimed that AHMO represented something vulgar.

From 1992–96, AHMO was absent for the most part from Wylie High School athletic events under the watch of head football coach Jimmie Brooks, though it was still seen and heard occasionally around Wylie.

According to Jon Peters, who coached the offensive line at Wylie under Coach Brooks, the Pirates were a team in transition in 1992. Coach Brooks kept on certain traditions but was still looking to change a few things, Coach Peters remembered. The Pirates had not been to the playoffs since Jerry Shaffer had left the school four years earlier.

At the same time, Coach Brooks was aware of the opponents' reaction to the AHMO mystique surrounding Wylie.

"AHMO almost became a battle cry for everyone else," Coach Peters recalled. "The big thing everybody else did, especially in Bonham and Commerce, was chant, 'No Mo AHMO,' and they really got it going. I think what Coach Brooks wanted to do was just not give 'em any ammunition."

When Mark Ball became the head football coach and athletic director at WHS in 1997, he brought AHMO back to the forefront, and it remains so to this day.

"I knew a little bit about Wylie football tradition from the '70s and the '80s, and obviously that's one of the things that was appealing about the job," Coach Ball explained. "I just feel like that's one of the things that when you're going in and you're trying to rebuild, I think one of the things you do is you draw upon tradition. I thought AHMO was one of the neat deals that Wylie had. Before me, they kind of didn't use it a whole lot. It wasn't important, I think. Some people told me they were trying to phase it out and not use it.

"I just felt like it was something that we needed to bring back, something our kids could draw upon," Coach Ball went on. "We needed to bring back any tradition that we could. That's really the basic reason that I want it to get back in our program and get it involved and give our kids something to take some pride in."

"I think at the time when Coach Brooks was here, (doing away with AHMO) was probably the right thing to do, because it did fire up other people," Coach Peters remembered. "One good thing Coach Ball did, I think, was resurrect that tradition."

AHMO has still got it. The dominating wins over Cleburne and Commerce proved that after more than a quarter century, AHMO was just as strong as ever.

"It makes you feel pretty good when you pass someone on the street," said Bob Skipwith, a 1978 graduate and the center for that state championship team, "or maybe someone will find out what it means and that you were playing when that came out, or you'll hear a conversation that, 'This is what that means.' Then you say, 'No, I was there when that story was originally told. I know exactly what it means.' I'm glad it's hung around. It's sort of a battle cry, and hopefully it'll hang around a while longer."

Coach Shaffer maintains that if someone would have asked him about AHMO the Tuesday following the Breckenridge game, he would have said it was temporary, though the ball was rolling—the night the players returned to Wylie from Weatherford after beating Breckenridge, the cheerleaders had already shoe-polished AHMO on the windows of many of the players' cars.

After the state championship game against Bellville, Coach Shaffer realized that AHMO was in Wylie to stay. For several years in the 1980s, it was featured prominently on the side of the Pirates' helmets during football games in place of the block "W" which they had favored for so long.

"One of the things that made it stick was we didn't have a change of coaching staff (after 1977)," the coach explained. "I stayed another several years, we went to the playoffs a bunch more times and we won a lot of other exciting games. It had a chance to not just sprout, but in order to take root and grow.

"You would have to kill several hundred thousand people to kill AHMO now," he continued with a laugh. "Maybe you couldn't even do it with that."

One such game where AHMO was in full force for the Pirates was against Frisco on October 24, 1986. This was a game that was played out toward the end of the season and had playoff implications. The Pirates trailed by four points with less than a minute left to play when Coach Shaffer called a timeout and used an old familiar strategy.

"I got to watch the game, I didn't have to scout that night," said Jon Peters, who was a coach at Wylie Junior High at the time. "We were down four points with just under three minutes left in the game. We got the ball and started marching it down the field. We had the ball on our 30 or 40 yard line. He called timeout and brought everybody over and literally drew the pass pattern in the dirt off a play action pass that we had."

The result was a game-winning touchdown pass from Jason Brown to Shannon Howard with 44 seconds remaining. Wylie escaped with the win over Frisco, 24-21.

"It was just the fact that (Coach Shaffer) was very calm and knew exactly what he needed to do," Coach Peters recalled. "You hear stories about how a coach would draw something up on the sideline to win a game, and I saw it firsthand. It was pretty fun."

Phil Lemons, who played offensive tackle on the state championship team, put it this way: "When you mention Wylie to anyone who knows anything about high school football, AHMO will be associated with it."

The Years Since

One never knows when the opportunity to win a state championship might arise again. For some schools, that chance never comes even once. For others, like Plano, the opportunity to win state came often.

"I didn't know (Wylie winning state) was such a big deal at the time," said Macklyn Stripling, a longtime English and Art teacher who was new to Wylie in 1977. "I thought people did that all the time."

It was such a big deal in Wylie that on one school day, soon after the Pirates brought the title home, Principal Grady Burnett—who had been the head football coach at Wylie High School for most of the 1960s—dismissed everyone in the high school immediately after the teachers checked their rolls and gave all administrators and students the day off as a reward for the team winning state, according to Mrs. Stripling.

It turned out the Wylie Pirates and their fans did not have to wait long for the opportunity to win the state title again. The wait lasted one year, to be exact. The Pirates graduated 16 players from their 1977 state championship team, but had enough depth and experience returning to reach the state final again in 1978.

The 1978 season did not begin favorably for the Pirates. They were riding a 12-game win streak from the year before, but that promptly ended when Lancaster defeated them, 27-14, in a downpour at Pirate Stadium to open the 1978 campaign.

But just like the year before, the Pirates regrouped and won the next 13 games in a row—a team record—to reach the state championship game.

The win streak did not come easy, especially when it got to the playoffs. To win that 13th consecutive game, the Pirates had to knock off a familiar opponent—Childress—which they again defeated in the semifinal game, this time by a 12-7 score. This game was so physical that Rock King, who was the Pirates' starting quarterback as a junior, could not recall *not* getting tackled by Childress defenders on any one play where the Pirates used the option play to hand the ball off.

"They planted me every time," Rock said. "Their middle linebacker was named Larry Eggers, and I won't ever forget him, because I lined up right across from him and looked him in the eyes before we took a snap. He was a tough guy, and those kids from Childress were probably the most physical team that I remember playing against year in and year out."

Coach Rick Page remembered of that contest against Childress: "I can tell you that 1978 game (against Childress) was probably the most physical game that I ever coached. Those two teams kind of had a grudge to settle, so to speak because of the previous year. They were all healthy. I really think that after that game, we were so banged up that it affected us in the game against Sealy. That was a tough, tough ballgame."

The game against Sealy—the only thing standing in the way of a second straight state championship for Wylie. The town of Sealy was already famous for its mattresses, but in the late 1970s, their high school football team featured the record-setting running back, Eric Dickerson, who rushed for 304 yards on 33 attempts in the state final against Wylie. The Sealy Tigers won, 42-20, over the Pirates to become the 1978 Class 2A Texas state champions. Dickerson went on to star for Southern Methodist University in Dallas as part of the famed "Pony Express," then set the single season rushing record in the NFL while playing for the Los Angeles Rams (2,105 yards in 1984). He was elected to the NFL Hall of Fame in 1999.

"He had it all," said Chuck Edge, who played against Dickerson in that game as a senior defensive tackle for the Pirates in the fall of 1978. "He was the complete package. He was tough inside and uncatchable outside. He had great moves. It was really frustrating because the defense didn't get blocked all night long. It looked like everybody was in position (to tackle Dickerson). He'd just cut back, or cut outside. He was all over the place."

Ironically, Rock King ended up playing baseball at Texas A&M University on the same team as Scott Abel, who was the quarterback for Sealy in that 1978 state championship game.

"Scott remembered that game, and we visited after I was at A&M about that," Rock recalled. "Of course, his perspective was a little different than ours. I remember us being in the game and having a chance to win. He remembers, you know, it was just a matter of time until Eric busted another one. It was fun to reminisce with him about that."

Wylie had three all-state players from that 1978 state runner-up team—Rickey Blackman at safety (he had moved from linebacker, where he played the year before for the state championship team), Chuck Edge at defensive tackle and Rock King at punter. Rickey had 18 interceptions for the Pirates in 1978.

The Breckenridge Buckaroos made it to the playoffs in 1978 but lost to Bowie in the first round, 14-6. In 1979, Breckenridge met Wylie again in the regional playoff game—but this time, the Buckaroos exacted revenge, winning over the Pirates, 21-19. In that game, the Pirate defense held Breckenridge off in the fourth quarter and forced a turnover, thus giving Wylie a chance to win late in the game. But the first of two fourth-quarter field goal attempts by Rock King, now a senior, sailed over the upright and was ruled no good. Rock's second attempt of the fourth quarter was a long-shot, desperation last-chance attempt, and it fell short, thus ending Wylie's season and giving Breckenridge the playoff win.

It was clear that the Breckenridge fans and players remembered 1977. Some of the Buckaroos players who were seniors in 1979 had been sophomores on that 1977 team and experienced the heartbreaking defeat at the hands of Wylie. One of those was Mike Funderburg.

"That was definitely on my mind," Mike recalled. "We had a real good nucleus with those four or five sophomores that started for three years, and the junior class behind us was loaded with talent also. We were really looking forward to playing them again. That was definitely a revenge-type deal. I remember I didn't hardly sleep the whole week, I was just so excited we were gonna get another chance to knock 'em off."

The Buckaroos were able to defeat Wylie, but in the next round, they lost to the eventual 2A state champion, Van, in the state quarterfinal playoff game. Actually, the two teams tied, 13-13, but Van won based on the most offensive penetrations. For Mike Funderburg, that loss to Van his senior year proved more heartbreaking than the one to Wylie in the regional playoffs two years earlier.

As for the people of Breckenridge, the 1977 regional loss to Wylie was still difficult for them to swallow many years after the fact, and they let Wylie players Jack Hirmon and Dale Morgan know about it during a hunting trip several years later.

"We go hunting out there, and we're not very popular," Jack said. "They've still got a bad taste in their mouth out there. We have a dove lease out there, and the first time we went hunting out there, they had a barbecue the night of opening day. They do a little backwoods country gambling stuff, and it's just a bunch of guys that have been hunting all day long. There's usually two or three hundred people out there. They found out we were from Wylie and we decided that it was best for us to leave, and that was 10 years after the event. They don't forget about things like that."

As for Childress, they lost again in the state semifinal in 1979, this time to Van, 13-9, the week after Van knocked out Breckenridge. Bellville did not reach the playoffs again for another five years after losing the 1977 state final to Wylie.

In the 1980s, Wylie made the playoffs six times (they became a 3A school in 1980 when the UIL added an "A" to each classification and created the 5A level).

In 1981, led by such standouts as Kyle Craighead, Blake Barry and W.C. Nix, the Pirates reached the state quarterfinal after tying Bowie, 0-0, in the regional game and advancing based on offensive penetrations (the one penetration that put the Pirates ahead came on a penalty, according to one of the players, Richard Edge). In the quarterfinal (third) round, however, Wylie lost out to eventual state runner-up Gilmer, 16-14. In 1982, the UIL began allowing two teams per district into the playoffs, and another round was added; now teams needed to win six games to win the state title. In the five years from 1983–87, the Pirates made the playoffs each year but were never able to advance past the second round.

Before the 1988 football season, Coach Shaffer left the Wylie Independent School District to become the athletic director of the Carrollton-Farmers Branch ISD just a few miles north of Dallas up Interstate 35. In his 14 years as head football coach at Wylie High School, his team had won 123 games, lost 41 and tied two for an impressive .741 winning percentage.

Coach Shaffer's departure signaled the beginning of the lean years for Wylie football. From 1988–91, their best record under Sam Terry for any one season was 4-6. From 1992–96 with Coach Jimmie Brooks at the helm, the Pirates' record was a combined 21-29.

It took the Pirates 15 years after Coach Shaffer left to return to the playoffs, and for much of that time, they did not come close. In 14 seasons from 1988–2001, the Pirates finished above .500 only three times.

The only time they came close to the making the playoffs during that period was in 1993, in Jimmie Brooks' second year as the team's head coach. The Pirates started off red hot at 6-0, but split the last four games to finish 8-2 and miss out on what would have been their first postseason action in six years. The Pirates went into the season finale needing a win over a familiar opponent—Ferris, whom Wylie demolished in the last game of the 1977 season. But the tide had turned in 1993, and the Ferris Yellowjackets won that season finale, 20-16. The Pirates finished in third place behind Crandall and Ferris, and the playoff drought continued.

The 1993 Pirates featured a true rarity for Wylie High School football—the team had two 1,000-yard rushers in Bryan Jett and Steven McKnight. It was the first time in Wylie's lengthy football history the team had featured two 1,000-yard backs in the same season.

In 1994, the Pirates moved up to Class 4A and went 4-6 under Coach Brooks. It was also in 1994 that a great rivalry with Highland Park, a perennial 4A playoff team, was born in Wylie. In 1996, the UIL began allowing three teams per district into the playoffs in Class 4A, but the Pirates were still struggling. In fact, they ended that 1996 season at 3-7.

The following year, Mark Ball was hired as head football coach and athletic director at Wylie High School to replace Coach Brooks and return Wylie football to glory. He was familiar with Wylie from his days as head coach in Whitesboro in the early 1990s. In fact, Wylie and Whitesboro had a one-sided football rivalry going in favor of Wylie for many years before Whitesboro finally pulled one out over the Pirates, 14-6, on October 4, 1991, when Mark Ball was Whitesboro's head coach. It came on Wylie's homecoming night and virtually knocked the Pirates out of the playoff hunt.

"I had great respect for Wylie and their program," Coach Ball recalled. "They had had great success and won the state championship. I had been playing them for a couple of years and knew a lot about their program and the success that they had. It was a big deal (for Whitesboro to beat Wylie). In fact, I remember after we won the game, our fans actually stayed out on the field and it took a while to run 'em off and get the lights turned off. It was a huge win for Whitesboro."

Improvement at Wylie under Coach Ball was not immediate—the Pirates won only four games his first three years at the head of the team, from 1997–99—but it still seemed eminent. Prior to coming to Wylie, Coach Ball had been a part of rebuilding high school football programs at Graham, Whitesboro, Lake Travis and Spring Westlake, all in Texas.

"I'd been through a couple of these before," Coach Ball said. "Every program I'd gone to as a head coach had been down, so I felt like I had some good experience there. I knew it was going to take a lot of patience. But you had everything in place (in Wylie). The superintendent (Dr. H. John Fuller), the administration and the Board of Trustees were all very supportive and willing to do the things it was going to take to get our program back. Our community was very supportive. Again, you're in a program where you can draw upon tradition. We had tradition here—we had won a state championship, and not very many in the state can claim that. We had all those things in place, and the other things is we had a plan, and we kind of tweaked our plan at the end of each year. But we didn't sway from our plan. We stayed to it."

One of the first steps Coach Ball took to try to revive the struggling Wylie program was to remind the kids of Wylie's tradition-rich football past, and the 1977 team in particular. His theme for Wylie's team in his first year (1997) was "Reflecting on the past and planning for the future."

"We talked about traditions and we talked about the past," Coach Ball remembered. "Our whole focus when I came here was to get this program back to the playoffs. So we talked about (the past) and tried to draw upon it. I recovered some pictures of the state championship team. The first year (1997) we brought 'em back and honored 'em (during halftime at a home game)...We had some guys in our community who were involved at the time and were on that team, so they were around a little bit. Early I tried to bring a lot of guys around and let 'em talk about things. Even though in our program we weren't ready, mentally or physically or any other way to be a playoff team at the time, I wanted to start talking about it and thinking about it and carrying that down every year."

What happened in Coach Ball's fourth year in Wylie was an amazing turnaround similar to the one experienced by the 1974 Pirates in Jerry Shaffer's first year. In 2000, led by the District 12-4A most valuable player of that year, running back J.T. Holsan, Wylie improved from 1-9 (their 1999 record) to 6-4. They did not make the playoffs, but they were over .500 and competitive, and it was only a matter of time before the Pirates would get back to the postseason. Like their counterparts who had coached at Wylie under Jerry Shaffer, the coaching staff under Mark Ball was an extremely intelligent and football-savvy group, led by offensive coordinator Billy Whitman and defensive coordinator Bill Howard.

In 2001, the Pirates experienced some tough luck, just as the 1993 team had—they went 8-2 but did not make the playoffs. In 2002, Coach Ball's sixth season as Wylie's head football coach and athletic director, the Pirates finished the regular season at 9-1 and were the district runner-up to Highland Park. Incidentally, those Highland Park Scots handed the Pirates their only regular-season defeat that year. But Coach Ball had accomplished what he had set out to do five years earlier—take the Pirates back to the playoffs.

On November 8, 2002, Wylie came through with a 21-14 comeback win over Poteet—their first-ever win over their longtime Mesquite rivals at the varsity level—in the final Wylie varsity football game at Pirate Stadium. Chuck Edge's youngest son, Ben, was a senior wide receiver for that 2002 team (Ben's older brother, Josh Edge, played for the Pirates and graduated in 2001). Ben Edge played in the final football game at the stadium to complete the circle; his father had played in the first game at the venue some 26 years earlier.

The Pirates needed three overtimes to beat Greenville, 43-37, in the 2002 bi-district playoffs on the familiar artificial turf of Garland's Homer B. Johnson Stadium (nee Memorial Stadium). The Pirates then knocked out Dallas Thomas Jefferson High, 38-20, in the area championship, played in Frisco. They slipped by Waco University High, 19-18, in Burleson in the regional semifinal game before losing out to two-time defending state champion Ennis in the state quarterfinal, 42-7, in the first Wylie game ever played at Texas Stadium—home of the NFL's Dallas Cowboys (Ennis failed to win a third consecutive title—eventual champion Denton Ryan eliminated them in the next round, which was the state semifinal).

In 2003, the Pirates finished the regular season with an 8-2 record and made the playoffs for the second year in a row, marking the first time they had made consecutive playoff appearances since they made it in five straight from 1983–87. They made it three rounds deep into the 2003 playoffs before being eliminated by Kilgore, 20-17, at Texas Stadium.

Both the 2002 and 2003 seasons ended a few games early, but the Pirates were on their way to returning to their 1977–78 glory, a period which to most people in Wylie is a fresh memory.

"Even when we meet now at 10-year class reunions or 20-year class reunions, it's like it was just yesterday. When you go back and see those guys, it's like you never left," Jack Hirmon said.

A four-month period in late 2002-early 2003 saw the passing of two important members of Wylie's 1977 state championship season. Running back Wayne Tyson, "Tottie," died of a heart attack at his home in Flower Mound, Texas, at age 43 on September 30, 2002, and on January 5, 2003, Coach Kenneth Ard died in Houston at age 56 from skin cancer. Many members of that championship football team from a quarter century earlier attended the funerals for both men to pay their respects and to remember them.

Tottie was one of the more popular students at Wylie High School. His senior year, in the spring of 1978, he was voted Mr. WHS by his fellow students. His older brother, Lanny Tyson, had played football for the Pirates before his graduation in 1976. The Pirates' 1977 state championship was one of Tottie's favorite topics to discuss, according to his younger brother, Glynn, a 1980 graduate of Wylie High School and a junior varsity football player for the Pirates as a sophomore in the fall of 1977.

"I don't know that he talked about much else," Glynn remembered. "That was the highlight of his life. He moved on and did a lot of great things after that, but that was still the highlight of his life."

"He loved to play," Glynn continued. "You couldn't stop him. He wasn't a very big guy, but he was very mean. When it came to playing football, nothing scared him."

Coach Shaffer recalled that Tottie gained most of his yards running inside because a lack of speed prevented him from running outside. Tottie played one of his finest games in the state championship against Bellville with repeated gains against the Brahmas using the counter dive play up the middle. For the most part, the Wylie offensive line effectively blocked Bellville's two star defensive players, Pettiette and Albert (both of whom went on to play for SMU) in that game, and defensively, Bellville could not adjust to the Pirates' repeated runs up the middle—particularly those by Wayne Tyson.

"Tottie was one of those guys that could run inside," Coach Shaffer said. "He was one of those guys that everybody liked. Extraordinarily popular, very bright…that he died like he did is a flat-out tragedy. I wish that intervention of some kind could have occurred.

"Tottie pretty much typified what we played with. We played with people who wanted to succeed and were willing to do whatever they could possibly do to succeed, they could play whatever role it was they were going to play, and play the very best they could and support everybody else in the process. People call that teamwork, or unselfish, but that typified this group."

Center Bob Skipwith, who was a senior on the 1977 championship team with Tottie, said, "Wayne Tyson was one of the guys that epitomized our team—he did whatever it took. He had a big role our junior year on varsity. Our senior year, he got a lot of playing time, but it wasn't as much as he had the previous year. But Wayne was the kind of guy that said, 'Hey, whatever it takes. Whatever the team needs is what I'm willing to do.' That was a good thing. There were guys out there like that. It wasn't, 'Me, me me.' It was, 'What does the team need? If it needs me standing on the sideline cheering, then that's what I'll do.'"

Standing on the sideline cheering was something Tottie did enthusiastically during games when he was not playing, so perhaps it was only fitting that he and Jack Hirmon were given the award for the Most Spirited Players on the team in 1977 at the end of the season banquet. Jack recalled, "We don't keep in contact with each other, especially the seniors. But I think we're all still pretty close, and I think you could see that when Wayne passed away. Everybody who could have been at the funeral was there, and that would have been real important to him."

Like Wayne Tyson, Coach Ken Ard was extremely popular among the students at Wylie High School. When Coach Ard came to Wylie in the early 1970s, he was a Vietnam veteran in his mid-20s and was still learning the ropes of coaching football. Before moving to Wylie High in 1976, Coach Ard had coached at Wylie Junior High and had coached many of the juniors and seniors from the 1977 championship team when they were in junior high.

In fact, Coach Ard headed up the seventh grade football team at Wylie Junior High in 1972, while the high school varsity team was going 1-9. That seventh grade team lost only one game—to Van, by 14 points, according to Ronnie Cross. In the week following that loss to Van, the seventh grade Pirates did everything in 14s in practice—14 laps, etc.

More than 30 players suited up for that seventh grade team in 1972, but only 14 of them still played football in Wylie five years later when they were seniors.

Perhaps that seventh grade team's success was a foreshadowing of things to come five years down the road. And perhaps Coach Ard was the first one to see what that group of seventh graders could become in five years. Perhaps Coach Ard saw something in that team that no one else saw early on.

"It was during our seventh grade year," said Roy Fuentes, who was on that team. "I can't remember if it was at the beginning of that season, or toward the middle, but he made the comment that someday we'll win the state championship. And when he made that comment, it was just like, 'How did you come up with that idea?'"

It turned out it was not such a crazy idea after all.

Tony Garner remembers when Coach Ard, addressing the team before the state championship team against Bellville, recalled making that statement to the team years earlier.

"He said, 'You guys have the ability, as a team, to win state,'" Tony said. "Coach Ard said that. Four years later, we're sitting under the bleachers at Floyd Casey Stadium (in Waco), and he sat in the corner and grabbed all of us seniors over, and tried to get that out and couldn't. That was pretty cool."

In the fall of 1977, Coach Ard was in his second year with the high school varsity team. His responsibilities with the varsity team lay mostly with coaching the offensive tackles and defensive tackles that year.

"Coach Ard was the kind of guy that was extremely enthusiastic," said Bob Skipwith, a senior in 1977 who played football for Coach Ard at Wylie Junior High in the early 1970s. "Loved the game, loved the kids…he had a good understanding of the game, but he was a better technician than a big picture type guy. He really cared. He was genuine, very sincere. His enthusiasm more than made up for any lack of football knowledge. He was one of those that as a coaching staff, you like to keep around because he never turned you down or told you no.

You told him what you wanted done and he got it done. I think every program needs one those guys."

Coach Ard's enthusiasm for his job was contagious and had an extremely positive effect on the other Wylie coaches as well as the players, according to Coach Shaffer.

"You could call him kind of the 'glue' of the organization," Coach Shaffer recalled. "He made everybody else's job easier. He made everybody else's job more pleasant, because if there were rough spots and he could observe it, he smoothed them out if he could. He would accept the least pleasant tasks to do and do them willingly and set an example…he was just about the most unselfish person you could ever possibly imagine. You've got a guy like Ard, he sets an example in that locker room for everybody, the kids pick up on it, the coaches pick up on it and it's an attitude of unselfishness and willingness to do whatever is necessary."

Coach Shaffer became closer with Coach Ard as the years passed, and the two remained in touch after Shaffer left Wylie in 1988. Coach Ard lived in Decatur, Texas, at the time of his passing. Shaffer called Coach Ard's death "a great loss for humanity."

Coach Ard worked in the Wylie Independent School District for more than 20 years. By 1977, Coach Ard was one of the longest tenured coaches in the Wylie ISD, having coached there for more than five years. He was also the last of those 1977 high school coaches to leave the Wylie ISD, staying on until the early 1990s and bringing his enthusiasm to scores of other high school athletes, coaches, teachers and students.

"Over the years, he made sure it all came together as far as handling the equipment and being prepared to play," said Jess Croley, a senior defensive end/offensive tackle for the state championship team and another Pirate who played for Coach Ard in junior high. "He made sure all the uniforms were right, and plus he had his coaching job to do. And he was a part-time trainer, too…He was a big part of it. In fact, he was one of the bigger parts of it."

Coach Ard left a lasting impression with the students of Wylie High School not only as a coach, but as a teacher as well. For much of his time at WHS, he taught science subjects.

"Coach Ard was an incredible man, not only as a coach but as a teacher as well," said Debbie Tyson (formerly Dillon), who graduated from WHS in 1979 and later married Glynn Tyson. "I had him three different years in both middle school and high school combined and never had him as a coach and I respected him so highly as a teacher and as a person. He was tough, but we always knew he truly cared about each of us individually and wanted what was best for our future. He always showed a genuine interest in what was going on in our world. He truly cared about teaching biology as well. When he was in the classroom, he was in the classroom—both physically and mentally, which is sometimes unusual for a coach of an award-winning football team. He gave whatever he was doing at the time—his all."

Macklyn Stripling, a longtime teaching colleague of Coach Ard, said, "I admired him a lot. He was extremely enthusiastic…We had a teacher's work center, and he would come out shouting, 'Take no prisoners!' to get us all fired up. That and 'If you can't teach 'em, test 'em' were his favorite sayings. He was always smiling. He was just a great man."

Perhaps the passing of Wayne Tyson and Coach Ard at such young ages reminded everyone how fragile life is and how swift it can end, and how human we really are. Enjoy life while it lasts, because it is short and could end at any moment.

This group of Pirates did exactly that. One afternoon in Waco, Texas, capped an unlikely run to the top by a high school football team located in Southern Central Collin County, the Wylie Pirates. For one season, which ended with that marvelous afternoon in Waco, the Wylie Pirates were the best in Texas.

"We wrote down goals at the start of that season. We had to do three team goals and five individual goals. We didn't open those envelopes until the end of the year, and when they were opened, every one of them said 1977 state champions," Ronnie Cross explained. "So we were on a mission whether we knew it or not. That was our ultimate goal, and that's where we wanted to be.

"Every kid that plays high school football ought to be able to experience something like that. That's not realistic, and that ain't gonna happen, but every kid who plays high school football ought to be able to experience that feeling, that moment."

Jess Croley said of the Pirates' run to the title, "There were a lot of things that happened there. A lot of luck. They say luck is what happens when preparedness meets opportunity. We had good coaches, some good motivators and a bunch of kids that set some goals at the first of the year and worked really hard to attain them."

Rock King has been a part of many athletic teams since that year, both in college at Texas A&M and on the sidelines as a trainer with many high school football teams in Texas, including Wylie in the early 1990s. One of those football teams for which Rock was a trainer, Celina, won several state titles, and another,

Van Alstyne, reached the state championship game in 2001 before losing to Blanco.

"Having been a part of those things, I realize how special that group of players and coaches was that won the state championship (in Wylie)," Rock said. "It never would have happened again in a million years with the talent that we had on that team. It was just one of those things where the stars came together. (The coaches) made us believe in a way that we certainly wouldn't have been able to achieve without them."

Jerry Shaffer summed up the impact of the Wylie Pirates' 1977 state championship season by saying simply, "Those little things changed a lot of people's lives, careers, the directions they went. It influences people's attitudes forever when they have that magnitude of success or that magnitude of an event in their life. That's something they don't ever forget, and something I've hearkened back to countless times."

In fact, Coach Shaffer made a prediction to his players that someday, his players would meet people while on business trips out of town that would say, "That's the town that can play football," upon finding out the former player was from Wylie. Phil Lemons had such an experience nearly 10 years after Wylie won the state title, while on an airplane headed from Arizona to Dallas. Phil was seated next to former Arizona State All-America halfback and former Chicago Bears halfback Wilford "Whizzer" White, father of then-Cowboys quarterback Danny White. Whizzer was heading into Dallas to see his son play.

"It's almost like a make-believe story, but it wasn't," said Phil, who still works as an official at high school football games in Texas. "We were flying back, and we were talking football. He said, 'I can't remember the name of the town, but this town is just fanatic over football. Every Friday night, everybody's at the game. When they go the playoffs, pretty much they roll up the streets and turn out the lights...I can't remember what they say, but they have some kind of chant.' The more we talked, I figured out quick who he was talking about. I said, 'Was it Wylie?' He said, 'Yeah.'"

Indeed, it had to be Wylie.

The home of AHMO.

The 1977 Wylie Pirates

No.	Name	Position	Weight	Class
3	Collins, Wendell	RB	140	Senior
9	Cross, Ronnie	QB	145	Senior
10	King, Rock	K-P-QB	163	Sophomore
17	McClendon, Roy	FL-DB	150	Junior
18	Whitehead, Mark	TE-LB	177	Junior
20	Morgan, Dale	RB-CB	158	Senior
24	Blackman, Rickey	RB-LB	164	Junior
25	Tyson, Wayne	RB	150	Senior
31	Mayberry, Wayne	RB-DB	160	Senior
35	Garner, Tony	FL-DB	153	Senior
37	Cox, Randy	RB	140	Junior
46	Whitt, Dan	RB	150	Junior
48	Cryer, Bruce	QB-LB	150	Junior
49	Gollahon, Doug	TE	164	Senior
50	Adams, Kevin	C-K	165	Junior
52	Pelton, Tim	C-DT	174	Junior
55	Croley, Jess	OT-DE	201	Senior
58	Skipwith, Bob	C	165	Senior
60	Lemons, Phil	OT	190	Senior
62	Edge, Chuck	OG-DT	170	Junior
63	Schultz, Danny	OT-DE	178	Senior
65	Hughes, Jimmy	OG	152	Junior

AHMO Power

66	Wallace, Lon	OG	167	Senior
67	Jones, Russell E.	OG	185	Sophomore
70	Taylor, Gary	OT	165	Junior
75	Helm, Mike	OG-DT	172	Sophomore
77	Russell, James	OG	140	Sophomore
78	Wright, James	OT	180	Sophomore
79	Adams, Paul	OT	200	Senior
80	Hirmon, Jack	FL	143	Senior
83	Ripple, Troy	FL	124	Senior
84	Touchstone, Garth	TE-LB	184	Junior
85	Fuentes, Roy	FL-DB	154	Senior
87	Marshall, Mike	FL	145	Junior
88	Winters, Chris	FL	140	Junior

Joey Kirbo, Johnny Kirkpatrick, Danny Leopard, Russell T. Jones, Chris Gray, Bret Burleson, Steve Clemmons, Jim Chaney, Brent Coleman, David Honzell, David Howard, Bo Keller, Brad McDonald, Jerry McDowell, Mike Taylor, Grant Thomason, Gary Turner
Student Manager—Richard Powell
Head Coach—Jerry Shaffer
Assistant Coaches—Bruce King (secondary, receivers), Rick Page (defensive line, offensive line), Kenneth Ard, Dick Matkin, Bob Wyksop, Ron Thomas, Loy Dorsey, Roy Gollahon

Wylie Pirates 1977 Game Results

Date	Opponent	Site	W/L	Score
September 2	FW Diamond Hill	Wylie	W	53-14
September 9	Kaufman	Kaufman	L	53-33
September 16	Farmersville	Farmersville	L	14-12
September 23	Justin Northwest	Wylie	W	30-0
September 30	Cedar Hill*	Wylie	W	15-6
October 7	Midlothian*	Midlothian	W	23-6
October 14	Open			
October 21	Allen*	Wylie	W	37-10
October 28	Red Oak*	Red Oak	W	52-0
November 4	Forney*	Wylie	W	17-14
November 11	Ferris*	Ferris	W	34-0
Bi-district Championship				
November 18	Granbury	Weatherford	W	16-14
Regional Championship				
November 25	Breckenridge	Weatherford	W	12-10
State Quarterfinal				
December 2	Mount Vernon	Mesquite	W	35-10
State Semifinal				
December 10	Childress	Wichita Falls	W	27-7
State Championship				
December 17	Bellville	Waco	W	22-14

* Denotes District 12-2A game

Playoff game capsules

Wylie 16, Granbury 14

Bi-district playoff @ Weatherford Friday, November 18, 1977

Wylie	6	3	0	7	-	16
Granbury	7	0	7	0	-	14

	Wylie	Granbury
First downs	18	16
Yards rushing	145	100
Yards passing	107	133
Punts-average	40	35
Fumbles lost	1	1
Yards penalized	85	65

Granbury—Gene Sledge 35 interception return (Ronnie Myers kick)
Wylie—Ronnie Cross 1 run (kick failed)
Wylie—Rock King 27 field goal
Granbury—Tommy Holmes 1 run (Myers kick)
Wylie—Doug Gollahon 6 pass from Cross (King kick)

Wylie 12, Breckenridge 10

Regional final @ Weatherford Friday, November 25, 1977

Wylie	0	0	0	12	-	12
Breckenridge	7	3	0	0	-	10

	Wylie	Breckenridge
First downs	15	14

Yards rushing	97	221
Yards passing	139	12
Comp-Att-Int	16-35-0	1-4-1
Punts-average	4-32	4-31
Fumbles lost	1	3
Yards penalized	40	72

Breckenridge—Wade Stanford 1 run (Mike Funderburg kick)
Breckenridge—Funderburg 25 field goal
Wylie—Roy McClendon 17 pass from Ronnie Cross (pass failed)
Wylie—Roy Fuentes 30 pass from Cross (kick not attempted)

Wylie 35, Mount Vernon 10

State quarterfinal @ Mesquite Friday, December 2, 1977

Wylie	7	12	16	0	-	35
Mt. Vernon	3	7	0	0	-	10

	Wylie	Mt. Vernon
First downs	15	12
Yards rushing	121	172
Yards passing	224	38
Comp-Att-Int	11-19-0	5-13-3
Punts-average	4-41	4-20
Fumbles lost	2	1
Yards penalized	22	28

Wylie—Wayne Mayberry 19 run (Rock King kick)
Mt. Vernon—David Cates 34 field goal
Mt. Vernon—Brad Lowry 1 run (Cates kick)
Wylie—Wayne Mayberry 1 run (pass failed)
Wylie—Ronnie Cross 16 run (kick failed)
Wylie—Safety, Cates fumbled in end zone

Wylie—Doug Gollahon 56 pass from Cross (King kick)
Wylie—Garth Touchstone 37 pass from Cross (King kick)

Wylie 27, Childress 7
State semifinal @ Wichita Falls Saturday, December 10, 1977

Wylie	0	7	10	10	-	27
Childress	0	0	7	0	-	7

	Wylie	Childress
First downs	22	11
Yards rushing	231	186
Yards passing	78	53
Comp-Att-Int	9-17-0	4-14-5
Punts-average	4-39	2-34
Fumbles lost	1	3
Yards penalized	30	38

Wylie—Wayne Mayberry 8 run (Rock King kick)
Childress—Jim Eason 1 run (Kenny Dean kick)
Wylie—King 32 field goal
Wylie—Ronnie Cross 15 run (King kick)
Wylie—King 26 field goal
Wylie—Bruce Cryer 10 interception return (King kick)

Wylie 22, Bellville 14
State final @ Waco Saturday, December 17, 1977

Bellville	8	6	0	0	-	14
Wylie	7	8	7	0	-	22

	Bellville	Wylie
First downs	14	18
Yards rushing	318	217
Yards passing	113	152

Comp-Att-Int	6-11-2	9-14-1
Punts-average	4-31	6-34
Fumbles lost	3	2
Yards penalized	50	49

Wylie—Doug Gollahon 9 pass from Ronnie Cross (Rock King kick)
Bellville—John Jackson 46 run (Allen Ward run)
Wylie—Gollahon 42 pass from Rock King (Cross pass to Gollahon)
Bellville—Parker 35 run (run failed)
Wylie—Roy Fuentes 12 pass from Cross (King kick)

Individual leaders

Rushing—Bellville: Allen Ward 26-167, Rusty Parker 9-72, John Jackson 11-60. Wylie: Ronnie Cross 21-93, Wendell Collins 20-58, Wayne Mayberry 2-25.
Passing—Bellville: Rusty Parker 5-10-2-75, Allen Ward 1-1-0-41. Wylie: Ronnie Cross 7-12-1-111, Rock King 1-1-0-41.
Receiving—Bellville: Gary Travis 5-106, Virgil Anderson 1-10. Wylie: Doug Gollahon 2-50, Roy Fuentes 2-42, Garth Touchstone 2-26.

Index

A
Abel, Scott 145
Abilene 93
Abilene Wylie High School 79
Adams, Kevin vii, 21, 55, 84, 85
Adams, Paul vii, 16, 21, 61, 68, 135
AHMO xiii, 94, 95, 101, 103, 106, 108, 112, 121, 140, 141, 142, 143, 155
Albert, Paul 118, 120, 128, 133
Alexander, Paul 56, 57
Allen xvi, 50, 51, 52, 53, 56, 117, 120, 126, 159, 164
Ammerman, Jeff 5
Anderson, Ricky 115
Anderson, Virgil 164
Angelo State University 135
Ard, Ken vii, 13, 17, 25, 61, 151
Arizona State University 155
Arkansas, University of 130
Ashley, Antyonne 56
Associated Press, The 9, 31, 32, 37, 41, 113, 118
Austin College 12, 25, 135

B
Ball, Mark 141, 148, 149
Barrow, Kendall 133
Barry, Blake 147
Baylor, Jackie 3
Bedell, Sandy 52
Beeville 12, 31
Bellville xvi, 17, 23, 74, 77, 78, 79, 80, 81, 87, 94, 113, 117, 118, 119, 120, 121, 122, 123, 124, 125, 126, 127, 128, 129, 130, 131, 133, 134, 136, 142, 147, 151, 152, 159, 163, 164
Benson, Red 2
Birdsong, Charles 2, 3
Bishop, Bobby 38, 39, 40, 41, 131
Blackman, Rickey vii, 18, 19, 20, 21, 31, 32, 34, 36, 39, 42, 46, 48, 49, 61, 63, 64, 85, 89, 93, 95, 96, 97, 106, 110, 111, 114, 122, 125, 126, 127, 133, 135, 138, 145
Blanco 155
Bonham 141
Bostic, Jacklyn 69
Bowie 8, 9, 31, 93, 97, 102, 114, 146, 147
Breckenridge 60, 72, 87, 88, 91, 92, 93, 94, 95, 96, 97, 98, 99, 100, 101, 102, 103, 104, 105, 106, 107, 108, 111, 112, 117, 119, 121, 123, 124, 125, 129, 131, 136, 142, 146, 147, 159, 161, 162
Brenham 133
Brooks, Jimmie 141, 147
Brown, Jason 143
Burger, Reese 120, 126
Burleson vii, 12, 14, 15, 23, 134, 150, 158
Burleson, Bret vii, 158
Burnett, Grady 2, 3, 137, 144
Burris, Tom 5

C
Campbell, Earl 130
Carrollton-Farmers Branch ISD 147
Cates, David 108, 110, 111, 162
Cavanaugh, Artis 96, 98, 100, 103
Cedar Hill 45, 46, 47, 48, 159
Celina 154
Chaney, Jim vii, 158

Chicago Bears 155
Childress 9, 112, 113, 114, 115, 116, 117, 119, 129, 131, 133, 144, 145, 147, 159, 163
Christopher, Ken 2
Cleburne 141, 142
Clemmons, Dianne 71
Clemmons, Russell 2
Clemmons, Steve 158
Clemmons, Wayne 2
Click, Bobby 2
Coleman, Brent 158
Collin County xv, 7, 30, 50, 130, 131, 132, 154
Collins, Wendell vii, 18, 32, 35, 40, 51, 55, 57, 58, 61, 63, 77, 78, 84, 85, 89, 90, 97, 99, 100, 101, 108, 116, 132, 138, 164
Commerce 26, 141, 142
Cooper 131
Couch, Chris 57
Cox, Randy vii
Cozart, Rocky 97
Craddock, Mike 39
Craddock, Tony 38, 39
Craighead, Kyle 147
Crandall 147
Croley, Jess vii, xvi, 13, 16, 17, 19, 21, 29, 34, 43, 48, 61, 68, 75, 101, 110, 121, 125, 127, 128, 132, 133, 135, 138, 153, 154
Cross, James 2, 11
Cross, Ronnie vii, 11, 18, 23, 26, 27, 30, 31, 32, 34, 36, 39, 42, 48, 52, 53, 54, 55, 56, 61, 62, 63, 77, 78, 84, 85, 89, 90, 91, 96, 99, 100, 101, 104, 106, 108, 109, 111, 113, 114, 115, 116, 119, 123, 126, 127, 128, 131, 132, 133, 134, 135, 137, 138, 152, 154, 161, 162, 163, 164
Crowley 3, 8, 12
Cryer, Bruce vii, 22, 36, 37, 54, 55, 73, 80, 87, 88, 109, 114, 115, 138, 157, 163

D

Dallas Cowboys 40, 105, 107, 113, 150
Dallas Thomas Jefferson High 150
Dallas Times Herald 134
Dean Martin's Celebrity Roast 94, 140
Dean, Kenny 133
Decatur 153
Denton 8, 150
Denton Ryan 150
Diaz, John 32
Dickerson, Eric 134, 145
Dodd, R.C. 2, 8
Dorsey, Loy 158
Douglas, Buster 94
Downing, Dale 61, 63, 65
Duke, The 119
Duncan, Greg 51
Duncanville 4

E

East Texas State University 26
Edge, Ben 149
Edge, Chuck vii, 10, 17, 20, 21, 23, 26, 46, 48, 49, 54, 56, 61, 81, 87, 95, 96, 98, 103, 106, 110, 116, 119, 132, 134, 138, 145, 149
Edge, Josh 149
Edge, Richard 147
Eggers, Larry 144
Ennis 150

F

Farmersville 2, 3, 5, 7, 30, 37, 38, 39, 40, 41, 42, 44, 51, 86, 100, 116, 126, 131, 132, 159
Feagin, Sue Ann 71, 75
"Flea flicker" 39, 100
Flores, Mike 32
Flower Mound 150
Floyd Casey Stadium 152
FM 544 137

Index

Forney 5, 6, 7, 8, 55, 56, 57, 58, 60, 84, 124, 159
Fort Worth Diamond Hill xvi, 30, 31, 44
Foster, Chase 136
Foster, Gary 5, 8, 11, 136
Fouts Field 8
Frisco 5, 7, 143, 150
Fuentes, Roy vii, 8, 18, 19, 20, 21, 26, 27, 31, 43, 51, 61, 63, 64, 65, 88, 91, 94, 97, 99, 100, 102, 104, 111, 119, 121, 122, 126, 130, 132, 152, 162, 164
Fuller, H. John 148
Funderburg, Johnny 93
Funderburg, Mike 93, 94, 96, 97, 99, 100, 104, 105, 106, 146, 162

G

Galleon, The 116
Garland vii, 8, 44, 88, 150
Garland Memorial Stadium vii, 8, 88
Garner, Tony 157
Gibson, Benji 4, 11, 140
Gibson, Brandon 140
Gibson, Chase 140
Gibson, Jesse 11, 140
Gilmer 147
Gollahon, Doug vii, 14, 16, 18, 23, 25, 30, 31, 32, 34, 35, 36, 40, 42, 47, 49, 52, 55, 57, 58, 61, 65, 90, 100, 101, 103, 105, 106, 108, 111, 123, 124, 132, 133, 134, 135, 138, 157, 161, 163, 164
Gollahon, Roy 14, 158
Granbury 8, 22, 86, 87, 88, 89, 90, 91, 94, 95, 101, 104, 112, 117, 119, 159, 161
Gray, Chris vii, 158
Green, David 2
Greenville 150
Grimes, David 51
Gurley, Danny 61

H

Haggerty, Dan 94
Hale, Mike 2
Hale, Rusty 69
Hardison, Nicky 115
Harris, Franco 105
Harrison Intermediate School 6
Hartman Elementary School 6
Hayworth, Gerald 89
Hayworth, Mark 89
Hazle, Tony 32
Helm, Mike vii, 21, 87, 95, 126, 158
Hicks, Joey 61
High Island 133
Highland Park 141, 148, 149
Highway 78 37
Hirmon, Jack vii, 21, 22, 27, 45, 61, 63, 65, 118, 120, 125, 128, 135, 137, 146, 150, 151, 158
Holmes, Tommy 89, 161
Holsan, J.T. 149
Homer B. Johnson Stadium 8, 150
Honzell, David 158
House, Gibby 56
Housewright, John 2
Houston, University of 4
Howard, Bill 149
Howard, David 158
Howard, Shannon 143
Hughes, Jimmy vii, 21

I

"Immaculate Reception," The 105
Interstate 35 53, 147
Iowa Park 130

J

Jacksboro 91
Jackson, John 123, 164
Jackson, Steve 125
Jerry Shaffer Stadium 137
Jett, Bryan 147

Jones, Roger "Peely" 34, 35, 91, 105, 134
Jones, Russell E. vii, 158
Jones, Russell T. 158
Jones, Zenford 51, 52, 53
Justin Northwest 7, 20, 43, 44, 45, 48, 70, 159

K

Kangaroo Stadium 87, 93
Kaufman 3, 7, 30, 33, 34, 35, 36, 37, 38, 41, 91, 107, 116, 120, 134, 159
Keller, Bo vii, 158
Kilgore 4, 150
Kimbrough, Tom 130, 134
King, Bill 5
King, Bruce vii, 10, 12, 15, 19, 21, 25, 26, 28, 31, 41, 43, 58, 61, 90, 92, 94, 98, 102, 103, 105, 106, 109, 110, 121, 123, 138, 158
King, John 13, 14
King, Rock vii, 9, 14, 20, 28, 31, 32, 33, 35, 36, 39, 42, 45, 47, 48, 49, 51, 52, 54, 56, 57, 61, 84, 88, 89, 98, 100, 104, 108, 111, 115, 116, 123, 124, 126, 129, 133, 134, 135, 138, 144, 145, 146, 154, 161, 162, 163, 164
Kirbo, Joey 158
Kirkpatrick, Johnny 158

L

La Grange 113
Ladylike Shop, The xv
Lake Lavon xv, 22
Lake Travis 148
Lampkins, Norman 49
Lancaster 144
Lee, Matt 39
Lemons, Phil vii, 12, 17, 22, 24, 26, 28, 42, 61, 77, 96, 98, 101, 103, 132, 139, 143, 155
Lemons, Sherry 69
Leonard 26
Leopard, Danny vii, 158
Leopard, David 13, 14, 15, 27
Life and Times of Grizzly Adams, The 94
Linden-Kildare 107
Linnstaeder, Jim 133
Lloyd, Gerald 3, 25
Los Angeles Rams 145
Lowry, Brad 108, 162

M

Marion, Steve 51, 52
Marshall, Mike vii, 138
Martin, Mayor William E. 107
Martinez, Robert vii, 138
Matkin, Dick vii, 25, 61, 158
Mayberry, Cody 140
Mayberry, Sheri 69
Mayberry, Wayne vii, 14, 18, 20, 21, 35, 36, 39, 40, 44, 45, 52, 53, 55, 56, 57, 58, 61, 63, 76, 77, 95, 100, 108, 109, 115, 116, 119, 122, 126, 128, 129, 132, 133, 135, 140, 141, 162, 163, 164
McCarley, Rhonda 69
McClendon, Roy vii, 18, 20, 21, 57, 61, 63, 65, 99, 114, 162
McCrary, Hardee 12, 25
McDonald, Brad vii, 158
McDonald, Phyllis 69
McDowell, Jerry 158
McKesska, Mike 121
McKinney 7
McKnight, Steven 147
Meek, Danny 5
Meeks, Ricky 61, 65
Meredith, Don 107
Mesquite Memorial Stadium 108
Mesquite Poteet 149
Miami Dolphins 119, 120
Midlothian 47, 48, 49, 50, 55, 117, 159
Minnesota Vikings 105
"Mojo" 95

Monday Night Football 107
Moore, Donald 133
Morgan, Dale vii, 18, 20, 21, 39, 45, 47, 49, 61, 63, 64, 73, 109, 110, 122, 127, 133, 146
Morgan, Peggy 69
Morren, Perry 113, 115
Mount Vernon 73, 91, 106, 107, 108, 109, 110, 111, 116, 117, 119, 124, 159, 162
Murphy, Audie 38
Myers, Ronnie 89, 161

N

Nall, Kenneth 2, 86, 87, 107
NFL xvi, 105, 119, 130, 145, 150
Nix, W.C. 147
"No Name Defense" 119
Nossman Field 34

O

Oakland Raiders 105
Odessa Permian 95

P

Page, Rick vii, 5, 25, 26, 46, 55, 60, 61, 81, 88, 125, 136, 138, 145, 158
Parker, Charlie 2, 3
Parker, Doyle 120
Parker, Richard 2
Parker, Rusty 120, 122, 124, 125, 127, 129, 133, 136, 164
Pearson, Drew 105
Pelton, Tim vii, 20, 22, 61, 95, 119, 133, 138
Pettiette, Joe 118, 120, 133
Pickett, Wilson 95
Pirate Stadium 7, 8, 18, 29, 34, 44, 56, 130, 136, 137, 139, 141, 144, 149
Pittsburgh Steelers 105
Plano xv, 7, 13, 51, 113, 130, 132, 134, 144

"Pony Express," The 145
Port Neches-Grove 130
Pottsboro 131
Powell, Richard vii, 61, 158
Princeton 30, 137
Pringle, Billy 56

R

Ratcliff, Robin 71, 75
Red Oak 53, 54, 55, 117, 159
Richards, Guylyn 75
Ripple, Troy vii, 21, 61, 63, 65, 68
Rockdale 113, 118
Rockwall 3, 4, 7, 30
Ross, Chris 134
Rowell, Ronnie 2, 3
Russell, James vii

S

San Angelo 135
San Diego Chargers 130
Sasse, Billy 2
Schiefer, Joey 2
Schultz, Danny vii, 19, 31, 32, 48, 49, 61, 85, 119, 125, 126, 133
Seabourn, Truman 1, 2
Seagoville 30, 31, 137
Sealy xvi, 133, 145
Seguin 135
Shaffer, Jerry vii, 1, 3, 4, 5, 6, 7, 8, 9, 10, 11, 12, 13, 14, 16, 17, 19, 21, 22, 23, 25, 26, 27, 28, 30, 32, 35, 36, 37, 41, 42, 43, 46, 48, 52, 55, 56, 58, 59, 60, 61, 66, 85, 87, 89, 91, 94, 95, 96, 98, 99, 101, 102, 105, 106, 107, 108, 109, 110, 111, 113, 114, 116, 120, 122, 123, 124, 125, 129, 131, 133, 134, 135, 136, 137, 139, 140, 141, 142, 143, 147, 149, 151, 153, 155, 158
Sherman 4, 12, 25, 135
Shinn, Kevin 39

Skipwith, Bob vii, 10, 16, 17, 22, 27, 42, 61, 68, 85, 93, 97, 103, 111, 119, 127, 129, 132, 135, 142, 151, 152
Sledge, Gene 89, 161
Smith County 130
Smith, Billy Ray 130
Southern Methodist University 107, 145
Splendora 133
Spring Westlake 148
Stanford, Wade 96, 99, 105, 162
Staubach, Roger 105
Stripling, Macklyn xvi, 144, 154

T
Tackett, Truman 2
Taylor, Elvin 39, 40, 44
Taylor, Gary vii
Taylor, Mike vii, 158
Terry, Sam 147
Texas A & M Commerce 26
Texas A & M University 145
Texas Lutheran University 134, 135
Texas Sportswriters Association 133
Texas Stadium 130, 150
Texas Tech University 118
Thomas, Ron 158
Thomason, Grant vii, 158
Thomason, Trent 5
Touchstone, Garth vii, 16, 18, 20, 21, 22, 31, 35, 39, 40, 45, 46, 52, 57, 58, 61, 65, 75, 87, 100, 111, 116, 119, 132, 163, 164
Trammell, Ronald 35
Travis, Gary 125, 126, 164
Troup 130
Tulane 12
Turner, Gary 158
Tyler John Tyler 130
Tyson, Debbie (Dillon) 153
Tyson, Glynn 122, 153
Tyson, Lanny 150

Tyson, Mike 94
Tyson, Wayne v, vii, 7, 18, 32, 40, 45, 47, 51, 52, 55, 57, 61, 63, 68, 82, 122, 126, 135, 136, 150, 151, 154

U
University Interscholastic League (UIL) 1

V
Van 146, 147, 152
Van Alstyne 3, 5, 7, 38, 155
Verdell, Howard 47

W
Waco 76, 77, 78, 121, 130, 150, 152, 154, 159, 163
Waco University 150
Wallace, Lon vii, 17, 61, 68, 132
Ward, Allen 120, 126, 164
Washington Redskins 119
Watkins, Wally 2
Watkins, Winston 2
Weatherford 87, 93, 101, 142, 159, 161
West Rusk 91, 107
White, Danny 155
White, Michael 141
White, Wilford "Whizzer" 155
Whitehead, Mark vii, 18, 20, 21, 32, 46, 61, 65, 73, 96, 110, 114, 115, 133
Whitesboro 148
Whitman, Billy 149
Wichita County 130
Wichita Falls 9, 113, 130, 159, 163
Wichita Falls Memorial Stadium 113
Wilcoxson, Mark 39
Winters, Chris vii, 116
Wittenburg, Mike 57
World War II 38
Wright, Darrell 5
Wright, James vii, 158

Wyksop, Bob 158
Wylie Sports Association 22

Y

Yeoman, Bill 4

Made in the USA
Coppell, TX
24 October 2021